CONQUERING
COMMUNICATION
IN ORGANISATIONS

ENDORSEMENTS

Modern-day communications can feel like a battlefield. So many platforms competing for the same audiences who already have a reduced attention span and digital info overload. Marion's book is a welcome lifeline where she's been incredibly generous in sharing not only tips and tricks, but consolidating current trends into one, time-saving space. If you haven't experienced the benefits of successful internal communications yet in your work then you really must read this book which is a trusty how-to guide with case studies and exercises. The Marion-effect makes you look like an expert even if you don't always feel it!

Sandi Sher, Marketing Manager at TSiBA Education, Cape Town

Marion has written a real winner. Whether you're a novice or experienced writer, if you're interested in dramatically improving your communication in the digital world, this book is for you. It's more than a book. It's a how-to reference guide that spans the whole spectrum of communication platforms. Marion understands the subtle difference between communication that achieves positive outcomes, and communication that not only misses the mark, but can lead to negative consequences. Packed with case studies, examples, exercises, and practical hints and tips, this book will have you reflecting and learning as it guides you step by step to become a more effective communicator.

Nick Christelis, Chief Executive, Nick Christelis & Associates

Marion is a maestro at demystifying the world of communications. She is an excellent teacher and offers practical solutions to seemingly complex scenarios. This book will transform any novice communicator, or even an experienced one who has developed bad habits, into a bold and effective professional whose every word, whether typed or spoken, hits the target every time.

Helen White, Director of Communications, Orbis International Africa

This book will teach others, as Marion has taught our communications staff over the years, how to use digital formats and communication to get themselves heard. As an NGO we need to ensure we get responses to our correspondence and interaction with our website.

Conquering Communication in Organisations – The Digital Way will give people the skills they need to make sure their work is clear, concise and easy to read. By embracing digital communication you have a very powerful vehicle to make your voice heard in this ever more cluttered technological world.

This book should become an organisation's go-to reference book on communications.

Zane Wilson, Founder and CEO of The South African Depression and Anxiety Group (SADAG)

Marion is a prolific writer and a great PR professional besides being a fantastic person with great charisma. The opportunity of working with her in Mauritius was just amazing. She carries a wealth of knowledge – both academic and practical – from the business world. Synthesising such a rich experience into this publication was the ultimate gift she could have offered all of us. I have no doubt those who believe in communication in this digital age will relish this book.

Amaresh Ramlugan, CEO at The Concreate Agency, Mauritius.

Technological advancements have brought a need for organisations to transform the way they communicate. Marion has provided a great 'how-to approach' in managing digital communications in organisations, highlighting issues to take note of in improving digital communications.

This book brings Marion's many years of experience in communications to bear on unpacking easy-to-understand new communication techniques. I greatly recommend that all communications professionals read it as it provides valuable information on how to streamline internal and external communications and can be used as a study guide.

Congratulations, Marion, for providing new thoughts on issues that hinder effective communication as well as providing practical methods for tackling those.

Dumisane Ncube, Academic Head, Edunetworks Business School

First published in 2018

ISBN: 978-1-86922-701-2 (Printed)
eISBN: 978-1-86922-702-9 (ePDF)

Published by KR Publishing
P O Box 3954
Randburg
2125
Republic of South Africa

Tel: (011) 706-6009
Fax: (011) 706-1127
E-mail: orders@knowres.co.za
Website: www.kr.co.za

Printed and bound: HartWood Digital Printing, 243 Alexandra Avenue, Halfway House, Midrand
Typesetting, layout and design: Cia Joubert, cia@knowres.co.za
Cover design: Marlene de Villiers, marlene@knowres.co.za
Editing & proofreading: Valda Strauss,valda@global.co.za
Project management: Cia Joubert, cia@knowres.co.za
Index created with TExtract / www.Texyz.com

CONQUERING
COMMUNICATION
IN ORGANISATIONS

The Digital Way

Marion Scher

publishing

2018

ACKNOWLEDGEMENTS

To all my clients, colleagues and friends whose experiences helped shape my thinking for the content of this book, particularly Daniel Munslow, Kate Johns, Kevin Welman and Solly Moeng. And to my family, who support and encourage me in everything I do.

TABLE OF CONTENTS

ABOUT THE AUTHOR

Award winning journalist and author, Marion Scher is one of South Africa's top freelance journalists, media consultants and trainers. Having worked in all three forms of media – radio, television and print, including online – Marion consults and trains for many of South Africa's leading corporates and government departments as well as media houses.

Successful communication is her passion and as she says: "No passion, no point."

FOREWORD by Robyn de Villiers, Burston Marseller

In *Conquering Communications*, Marion shares her years of experience in the field of communications in an easy-to-read and accessible way. Focusing first on the increasingly critical area of Internal Communications – recognising that the workforce of today is an organisation's most powerful vehicle for external stakeholder engagement and that through the efficacy of our internal communication we equip our workforce to carry out this role for us, either well or not so well – Marion then shares her practical guidance on best utilisation of all forms of the "written word".

Marion's years of experience as a journalist, educator and consultant to organisations in the area of effective communication are evident throughout *Conquering Communications*, which is a structured read, providing wisdom, guidance and practical, easy-to-understand and use lessons for all involved in the communications industry.

Marion has always stayed abreast of advances in the industry and she covers the move to digital in a practical and easy-to-grasp manner.

Knowing Marion and having worked with her over many years, this read also provided a number of smiles as I recognised situations we have been in together.

Robyn de Villiers
Chairman and CEO, Burston-Marsteller Africa. Burston-Marstellar is a New York based, global public relations and communications firm.

INTRODUCTION

The world of communication has literally been tipped on its head over the last few years. The reason, quite simply, is one word – digitalisation.

When you think most people receive their information and news from their mobile phones this starts to tell a story. One I wanted to enlarge upon.

As someone who spends a great deal of time training people in the communications field, I realised there was a need to shake up the industry and make industry players aware they need to do things differently. From emails to newsletters and annual general reports there is one common thread today – make it short and sweet so that people will read it.

Today's readers fall into three distinct categories – skimmers, scanners and readers – with the majority falling into the first two groups. People's reading habits have drastically changed, and now consist of flipping from web page to web page, Facebook post to news site, spending an average of around six seconds at each destination. This means that if your communication, including emails, doesn't grab them immediately, the chances of them reading it all the way through are very small.

The other big change in communication is the amount of visuals used today, whether infographic, video, animation or whatever means you can use to grab someone's attention for a minute or two.

This book sets out to offer insights and ideas on just how to look at today's world of communications, using examples and case studies to illustrate the chapters.

In keeping with my ethos of being concise and succinct, I'll just say enjoy the book…

SECTION 1 – INTERNAL COMMUNICATION

CHAPTER 1

INTERNAL COMMUNICATION – THE GLUE THAT HOLDS AN ORGANISATION TOGETHER

"Coming together is a beginning. Keeping together is progress. Working together is success." – Henry Ford

Who are your most important stakeholders? Many would answer their clients, customers or perhaps their shareholders. They would be wrong. Your employees are far more than just people who work for you. They're your brand ambassadors. The people behind your company's name and generally the first interaction the public have when they call your organisation. They're the people who make your company tick.

Effective internal communication creates understanding and helps grow your staff and their knowledge of your business, which can only be a good thing.

Look at highly successful organisations today and you'll find that nine times out of ten there's a strong link between well-managed communication and building real trust and respect with staff.

In the past internal communication has been the poor cousin of public relations, with the internal newsletter being the only source of company news. Today, without effective internal communications, you're at risk of hijacking – from the person in your company with the biggest mouth and ears.

Savvy organisations today use every possible means of communication with their staff from those on the factory floor to the people at the very top of the ladder. Everyone benefits from great communication and nothing works better to inspire and unite staff to reach company goals.

And remember, one size doesn't always fit all. You have to look at the different tiers of staff and communicate accordingly, which doesn't necessarily mean writing down to people. However what management needs to hear may not be the same as EXCO or the guys on the factory floor...

WHERE DOES SOCIAL MEDIA FIT IN?

For many companies the growth of social media has become equally an asset and a problem. But one thing's for sure – there's no running away from it. Companies today have no choice but to embrace it. By learning how to harness this for good internal communications instead of damaging employee relations, you can have a winning formula.

When you engage with your workforce they feel valued, involved and know they genuinely matter. Morale is boosted, productivity is lifted and people actually look forward to going to work every day. Even when things may be tough – or *especially* when things get tough – communication counts even more. Don't let the whisperers tell the tale. Make sure your lines of communication are wide open where it counts.

Different methods of internal communication

Many times in employee attitude surveys the one area that shows up as consistently low in the rankings is communication with management. Management is often taken aback at this, feeling they are in fact good communicators and that it must be the other guy who didn't get the message right…

Employees are rarely part of decision-making, even though these decisions have a direct effect on their work and lives. Just feeling part of what's going on in their workplace takes away any insecurity and does wonders for employee morale.

Where to meet

This can literally be online or in person. A lot depends on the size of your organisation. Some, and here I mean exceptional leaders, make time each day to talk to staff, not necessarily about work-related issues but more to get to know them and what's going on in their lives. This also makes them more comfortable if there's something they need to communicate.

Let's look at some different ways of reaching staff:

Emails

Some CEOs believe in sending personally written emails to employees on what they're thinking about and important topics for the business. Some encourage staff to communicate with them by email.

The problem here is: how long does it take before that person receives a reply? The golden number is 24 hours... The person who took the time to write that email wants to know they've been heard.

Chat rooms

Why should you have a team chat app? After all, everyone's already got WhatsApp or something similar. By having a team chat app you can keep each department or the whole company's communications in one place, making it really easy to have private or group chats. Everyone's a tap away.

A team chat can also double for conference and video calls, screen sharing, integration with cloud storage services and more.

One thing that has to be monitored in any peer-review situation is wars of words. This is firmly in the list of cons of peer review and although criticism or unhappiness with a situation needs to be aired as much as anything else, the speed and way it's dealt with is vital. Something that could start out as a small rumour could end up as a big crisis.

Team huddles

These can be daily or weekly just to discuss goals, challenges or operating plans for the day. A quick meeting with early-morning coffee would be perfect – especially with the boss supplying croissants…

Town Hall meetings – being seen and heard

Generally we hear about Town Hall meetings during political campaigns where politicians literally use town halls and other buildings to talk about their campaigns and strategies. Town Hall meetings are often the easiest way of reaching the most people at one time, even if these take place around the country wherever the company has workplaces.

It's one thing to send out a company newsletter, email or memo but seeing a real person up on a stage, where staff can see their face and feel their body language, does far more to build trust and credibility.

Much of the success of these meetings depends on the facilitator and presenters, and whether staff feel comfortable enough to ask questions without feeling intimidated. If the CEO, who is the public face of the company, doesn't feel comfortable in this scenario it might be necessary to get them some presentation training.

There's no set rule as to when these should happen – monthly, quarterly, whenever issues that concern your employees arise or when there is a need to talk about important happenings within the company or even its competitors.

They're as much about getting feedback from your staff as your giving them information and possibly reassurance – a two-way communication street.

It sometimes helps if staff are asked to send in some questions beforehand (possibly anonymously), that give the facilitator a feel of what's really needed in terms of answers.

One thing that's important at Town Hall meetings is keeping an open agenda, where whoever is running the meeting answers questions as honestly as possible, with private issues being dealt with separately.

This isn't a place for policy decisions to be made and if there are questions that can't be answered on the spot – say so. These then need to be sorted out and report-backs given if companies' credibility is to be taken seriously.

Above all, remember this is for the benefit of your staff who need to know they'll be listened to and are not just there to listen to a one-sided lecture.

When you post/send out a notice about this Town Hall meeting you could do an online survey to help you draw up an agenda by asking:

- What's working well in the company?
- What's not working so well?
- What are the greatest organisational challenges you see?
- How can we improve things?
- What would you like discussed at the upcoming Town Hall meeting?

Tips for planning Town Hall meetings:

- Keep the sessions small – rather offer several different dates for people to attend.
- Serve a meal and encourage company leaders to sit with employees to hear what they say.
- Use visuals – pictures and video – to grab your audience.
- Present awards – even fun ones – to, for example, someone who went above and beyond that month/quarter. They don't have to be expensive awards – the recognition in itself is enough.
- Encourage feedback through a follow-up survey.

Targeted sessions

For smaller companies or perhaps particular groups, using the same ethos as above for Town Hall meetings can work just as well for targeted sessions with appropriate leaders or owners of the message.

CREATING A CULTURE OF COMMUNICATION

Building relationships

Studies have shown that companies that not only encourage but lay the groundwork for peer relationships and camaraderie within the workplace find their employees more likely to want to 'go the extra mile' at work.

By encouraging employees to think about their fellow workmates and be willing to change their behaviour and method of communication you could find a very different atmosphere in the workplace.

Speaking up becomes important in relationship building but this also means getting quick feedback – not being ignored for weeks on end. Very often management or EXCO aren't even aware there's a problem or any conflict. If a problem is left to fester and be dealt with by the gossip mill, it can explode from a problem into a crisis overnight.

Consistency in messaging

Communication can't be sporadic. There has to be regular communication, not just when there's a crisis situation. By finding the best communication tool for your company and using an 'open door' policy you'll never lose track of what's going on within your organisation.

Effective internal communication needs

- Open two-way communication – often face to face

- Plain, jargon-free, to-the-point language

- Regular interaction

- Giving your staff the information they need – not keeping them in the dark

- The use of good communicators, both written and verbal

- Easily accessible mediums for all staff

- Transparency at all times

- Open-door policy – everyone who talks should also be aware of listening

- Knowledge sharing

- Monthly company-wide meetings

- Regular feedback
- Emotional support for difficult work

Benefits of good internal communication

- Increased productivity
- Higher chance of reaching organisational goals
- Ability to approach situations, problems, changes or crises proactively
- A shared vision and sense of ownership in the organisation
- More effective and responsive customer service
- Employees who feel valued and part of the story
- Smarter decision-making on all levels
- Reduced conflict between staff
- Higher employee retention

What closes communication doors?

- Departmental silos

- Outdated systems

- Bottlenecks

- Need-to-know basis information

- Red tape

- Them and us attitude

Internal communication tools

Today we're leaning closer and closer to a workforce that doesn't need to be in the same place at the same time to achieve their goals and objectives. So how do you make sure you effectively reach everyone and get feedback and answers when you need them? What should you be using? It can be one or a combination of the following:

- Email

- Telephone

- Instant Messaging

- Forums

- Blogs

- Twitter

- Facebook

- Instagram
- YouTube
- Intranet
- Newsletters

There's no one correct answer here – it's purely a case of what works for your organisation, depending on the size and character of your business. We'll be looking at these different types of communication in more detail throughout the book.

The dangers of working in silos

Having trained and consulted in many of South Africa's largest organisations, the single biggest problem in the world of internal and often external communications is silos! Much has been written on this topic with headlines such as: 'Tear down the walls'; 'Break down the silos'; 'Smash your silos' being used.

In his book, *Silos, Politics and Turf Wars*, business writer Patrick Lencioni says: "Silos – and the turf wars they enable – devastate organisations. They waste resources, kill productivity and jeopardise the achievement of goals."

My experience has shown that within a single organisation, groups of people are not only at 'war' with each other but are heading in completely different directions involving company policy and decisions. Not having a common goal and vision for an organisation can only lead to disaster, which is where the organisations I'm talking about have ended up.

In today's world of instant communication, with easy access to information, there should be no excuse for this situation.

Creating isolation

One company where I'd conducted writing training told me with glee how awful their public relations section was and indeed showed me this department's really bad media releases. When I offered to run the same courses I'd given this team to the PR guys, the response was a firm no, you can't. The reason being they enjoyed seeing this department fail…

Parastatals are particularly notorious for their silo mentality, with the various departments generally completely unaware of the organisation's initiatives if they don't concern them directly. The problem here is that without a single, qualitative focus, there can't be a single common goal. Only from the top can you encourage communication and trust throughout the entire company.

Rowing in the same direction

A unified goal has to start with buy-in from the very top of the organisation down. Everyone needs to be in the same boat going in the

same direction – from executives, through management and the teams under them. Very often the problem stems from leadership themselves not being united, with managers under them fiercely guarding their departments and almost being 'against' the rest of the organisation.

To change this behaviour needs leaders to come together and work to motivate all their employees towards a common goal. Does your department know what the other departments in your organisation are even working on? Does marketing know what advertising or research and development are doing?

When I give media training, for instance to heads of various departments, I often find they know each other by title but have never sat around a table together. They work around the same issues but don't know what the common message is around these issues. By the end of the day they have often laid the groundwork for future working relationships.

Some tips for interdepartmental relationships:

- Think tanks where people can talk about what they're doing and get input from other departments – the more heads, the more ideas

- Cross-departmental training encouraging constructive feedback

- Events such as lunch meetings giving company updates

- Town Hall meetings

- Video or conference calls

- Make sure information is shared across all departments and that no one is left out of the picture on what's happening in the organisation

- Share company stories around CSI projects, client successes. Each department has its own stories – make sure these are shared – with photos, where possible, to show how important everyone's contribution is

- COMMUNICATE, COMMUNICATE, COMMUNICATE – use intranet, internal newsletters, emails – whatever it takes to spread the company message

WATCH YOUR TONE

Not what you say but how you say it

Today, with people's fingers doing more talking than their mouths, messages can often go terribly wrong. Apart from predictive text turning your intended message into gobbledygook it's often hard for the person receiving the message to interpret the tone of the message. For instance:

"Received your report. Need to go through it with you urgently before anything gets sent out."

What does this mean? That your report isn't particularly good? That you've made a complete hash of it? Or perhaps this person just needs to get up to speed on it before it's sent out. The problem is, as you can't hear the message or see their body language or the tone of voice behind it, you're not sure what they mean. A common response to such a message would be "Stuff them. I put in so much work on that report and this is the gratitude I get…" So a better message would have read:

"Thanks for the report. Would it be possible for us to sit together as I'd just like to go through a few points before it's sent out?"

Such a small difference but it's all in the tone.

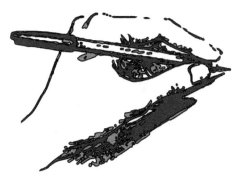

Writing in anger

So you're really angry and ready to fire off an sms, email or worse – a Tweet – around a company matter. Remember, once you press that button there's no going back. The other problem that we'll look at in more detail later is that once out there on the internet, that's it. The whole world can view your anger and when you cool down a few minutes or hours later it's too late to do anything about it.

CASE STUDY: Chris Moerdyk, Marketing Guru and Analyst

One of the biggest problems in any large company, particularly those that have factories or workshops attached, is being able to communicate with all staff particularly on the factory floor. And even more particularly in a multi-cultural and multi-lingual country.

The BMW Assembly Plant in South Carolina, USA had precisely this problem because many of the white collar and factory floor staff were from Puerto Rico, Mexico and Germany.

Newsletters and newspapers were ruled out simply because they took far too long in perpetration and the editors would be faced with enormous literacy problems.

The second challenge was to communicate with the workforce in a credible way. Perceptions among the staff of pretty much any big company, when they receive any form of communication from top executive or board level, is to treat the information they are being given as having been carefully vetted by the powers that be. On top of which there's always the frustration of not being able to question information that's being disseminated.

So a communication task group was formed to get to grips with these myriad challenges.

The answer came in the form of an internal radio station that was to be broadcast to all office staff via small loudspeakers or headphones. Factory workers could only listen to their radio if they wore their ear protection which had built-in radio receivers. Killing two birds with one stone among staff who tended not to wear their ear protection in spite of this being mandatory.

Then, for 55 minutes of every hour, staff could listen to outside music or talk radio stations of their choice in the language of their choice. These were simply radio stations in the area that were only too delighted to have additional listeners.

On the hour, every hour for one minute there would be a news report consisting of general regional and international news headlines followed by four minutes of internal company news. But, none of this internal news consisted of board members or top executives droning on about something but rather being interviewed and asked questions posed by staff.

The interviewer was an outside radio DJ employed by the company – but responsible to the workforce. He listened to their music and talk requests and, on their behalf, interviewed top executives on the corporate statements they issued.

The upshot was that staff took ownership of "their" radio station and suddenly the corporate statements from up top were perceived to be a lot more credible.

Interestingly enough the process of establishing an internal radio station on this model, is one of the least expensive methods of internal communication.

But best of all, it is instant.

On a lighter note **from Chris Moerdyk**

THE FASTEST INTERNAL COMMUNICATION EVER

At least once a month, the board of BMW South Africa in Midrand, would decry the problem of internal communication. The much vaunted "Cascade" system which saw messages laboriously working their way down the ranks from the board right down to the factory floor just wasn't working. Its failure was the reliance upon managers at various levels remembering to pass on information.

Being the communications executive on the board I was asked by my colleagues to try and come up with something that was quick and efficient.

We discussed the vagaries of human communication and how, in fact, human beings were Mother Nature's worst communicators.

Just before we broke for midmorning tea, after one of our weekly board meetings, I suggested as an exercise that our finance director wander about his department and casually mention to a known gossip: "Don't tell anyone but…" We'd chosen a board decision reached earlier that morning as our test message.

When we returned from our tea break we had bets on how long it would take for the message to travel through the gossip grapevine and reach the lowest ranks of those employed at head office.

Just before lunch, the marketing director's secretary came hurrying in to the boardroom and told him the BMW dealer in Port Elizabeth wanted to have an urgent word with him.

The marketing director came back laughing his head off. Our message had not only spread through the head office grapevine but had reached the ears of a dealer 1000 kilometres away in around an hour.

From that day on whenever we wanted to get important information across we would send it down the corporate grapevine choosing as our messengers the most active gossip-mongers.

While one might think this a rather silly method of corporate communication that has no serious role to play, it's extremely effective as long as it's used only when absolutely necessary and not frequently enough for the staff to catch on.

WHAT THE EXPERTS SAY ARE THE WORST PROBLEMS IN INTERNAL COMMUNICATIONS

Kate Johns, Head, Africa Communications at Standard Bank:

The first is badly written material that has zero relevance for the intended audience – and keeping in mind that there are numerous audiences in any organisation: executives have key requirements while sales or customer-facing staff has others. Too often we see general messages sent to all, resulting in limited traction and action. The second problem is an over reliance on email as the channel to communicate internally – I still think one of the best ways to get messages across (particularly important ones) is through town halls, or smaller/targeted sessions with the appropriate leaders or owners of the message.

Kevin Welman, Director, ByDesign Communications:

Communities, entities, organisations, governments etc., need to keep their audiences better informed. There is a much greater need for transparency today than ever before. We live in the information age, trust is earned and retained on transparency. In addition, organisations need to act in an authentic manner. They need to do what they say and say what they do. There simply cannot be a gap between their intentions and their actions.

Daniel Munslow, CPRP, Independent Communication and Brand Consultant:

Internal communications suffers from a disconnect between their function and other business units that deliver on the brand experience. Employees, especially in the service industry, understand the concept of service, but are let down by systems that prevent them from delivering on the brand promise. Reduction in silos and better collaboration between communications and business operations is urgently needed. Leadership is also not leveraged enough to engage employees face to face and human to human. Impact measurement is often lacking, preventing business case reporting to senior leadership.

Solly Moeng, Managing Director and Senior Consultant, DonValley Brand, Marketing & Communications Agency:

Organisations that function in silos, with people protecting internal turfs and making it hard for others to access information, expose themselves to potential reputational embarrassment. In fact, in the era of invasive digital media, 'internal' no longer exists. That's why what used to be the internal newsletter is today old fashioned because whatever is intended for internal ears only often ends up out there and given all sorts of unintended interpretations.

Communicators should therefore always assume that what gets disseminated internally will be shared with outsiders and could be used to embarrass the organisation. They should ask themselves "What if it ends up out there?" before pressing the send button, especially with electronic communication. Too little vertical information sharing – from *top down and bottom up – can also hurt the business, as ill-informed/ uninformed people might take operational action that might not be in line with broader executive or employee thinking/expectations, and face revolt/resistance.*

CASE STUDY: MAKARAPA CITY — TAKING THE STORY TO THE PEOPLE

When it comes to communication, no one has a harder time than the mining industry. When they make the news, it's rarely for a good reason. Take Marikana, for instance, or stories of miners' strikes and mine accidents. Few have anything good to say about mining companies, even the miners.

So when Anglo American, one of the main mining employers in South Africa, wanted to reach out to its staff and their communities in a way that would make a real difference, they chose the one medium they knew they would listen to – radio.

Reaching out to the communities

"We saw there was a trust deficit between mining companies and the communities they operate in, particularly around operations," explains Dr Pranill Ramchander, Head of Corporate Communication at Anglo American. *"The mining industry was changing and Anglo American was seen as a symbol of the sector's issues.*

There was a perception that mining wasn't doing enough for these communities around issues from health to housing and education. All of this in an environment of high unemployment.

"Although this trust deficit exists, we find employees who actually live in the communities have a different perception. We're a significant employer in these communities, and we're trying to make a bigger, more sustainable contribution than ever, accelerating programmes in health, education and enterprise development and local procurement that will upskill the unemployed. We provide a whole range of services and support."

Although service delivery remains primarily the role of local government and municipalities, Anglo American also partners with them on health and education programmes such as the Batho Pele mobile clinics and early childhood learning development.

Reaching hearts and minds

With these programmes up and running, Anglo American set out to develop awareness around them and to encourage participation. "The programmes are there for the communities and we need to reach people and get them to participate, improving their wellness in a number of areas," enthuses Ramchander.

"2016 saw the company announcing an asset disposal programme. Markets were tough and commodity prices weren't in good shape. Added to this, communities were protesting for better services, so it was a challenging time for us to communicate with them. We had to find an innovative way of reaching our communities, which brought us to this approach."

Opening communication doors

*"We needed to shift perceptions, behaviours and attitudes,"
explains Ramchander. "We want people to understand that Anglo
American is there to make a difference in their communities.
We needed to tell them about our initiatives and to change their
behaviour to achieve positive outcomes.*

*"We had to look at how we could do this in a more engaging
way without being intrusive or overbearing," says Ramchander.
"We chose storytelling as the best form of communication, and
a serialised radio drama as the drawcard. We used the power of
edutainment to educate and entertain, whilst locking the audience
in, so they come back wanting more."*

*Using various regional radio stations that spanned the languages
spoken by their communities they were able, for the first time, to
reach people in their mother tongues.*

*"We were speaking to our target market on their terms. Radio
drama is an emotional connection, reaching out to people's hearts
and minds. We looked at the areas we operate in and the most
spoken languages used there, which was how we chose the radio
stations, trying to cover all our employees. The show goes out in six
languages plus English," adds Ramchander.*

Makarapa city is born

And so Makarapa City, a fictitious mining town named after the miners' decorated hard hats, emerged, giving a glimpse into what affects mining communities.

"We have feuding families who experience various social economic issues – not just within their communities but South Africa as a whole," says Ramchander. "Although mining towns were our initial target market, we quickly realised we had even more listenership outside the mining community."

The show begins with a jingle so catchy you find yourself humming it the whole day, before a rich baritone voice tells you about Makarapa City:

> "Set in the exciting world of mining – the story revolves around a feuding family that pits brother against brother, even father against son."

The intended lessons for the community came acroos strongly in the drama series

EMPLOYEE INDEBTEDNESS	CONSEQUENCES OF ADULTERY	MINE COMMUNITY DEVELOPMENT/ ENTREPRENEURSHIP	TRANSFORMATION/ WOMEN EMPOWERMENT	HEALTH/ EDUCATION
• The dangers of using a loan shark i.e. high interest rates. • Financial wellness	• Increased risk of HIV/AIDS infection. • Financially strapping – supporting two families.	• Ways to alleviate poverty e.g. funding black start up business.	• Changing role of women as part of decision making • Grooming independent women • Youth • Procurement	• HIV/AIDS has no face. • Nurses can also get infected.

And so you're hooked. If that's not enough, stick around until the end of the show when you could be one of the lucky winners of a R500 shopping voucher – courtesy of Anglo American.

"The competition is a big drawcard," says Ramchander. "We get around 60 000 entries a week with over 50% having the correct answers."

With authentic characters going through the trials and tribulations of life the tales unfold of adultery, debt problems, work issues and promotions, family and health issues.

In one episode a father asks his wife why their daughter doesn't visit them more. The answer is simple. After going through various educational programmes and a degree, she's now a mining engineer. And, the mother informs him, "You see, women today can be educated and go as far as any man. It's a modern world now..." This kind of message helps break stereotypes.

"As well as educating the communities around schools, mobile clinics, HIV testing and employee indebtedness, we're also telling aspirational stories to encourage people to become involved in what's being offered to them," explains Ramchander. "We get a lot of enquiries around bursary funding, which they hear about on the programme. Many inquiries are from areas we don't operate in."

Makarapa City is a microcosm of what happens outside the mining community of South Africa. "We're highlighting in a specific space just what happens everywhere. We've also seen how we can make this far more effective than just radio. People also want that face-to-face engagement and this is where theatre comes in to reinforce the stories.

"Aside from being on radio, our office employees can also listen to the programmes on internal intranet. The show has also drawn large media attention, with articles in publications such as Finweek, *not to mention the public relations that come out of Makarapa City on Facebook and Twitter," adds Ramchander.*

Integrated communications approach to Makarapa City

Integration is key

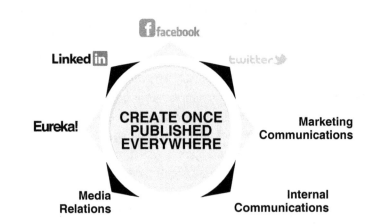

Research has also shown the programme to be far more cost effective than previous print campaigns, with the results showing:

- *97% enjoyment – found it positive and credible. Provided them with content to connect with the story*

- *87% changed their perception about the company – that it was good for the community, their education, health and early childhood education*

- *77% remembered it was Anglo American*

Makarapa City into the future

"Now in its third series, the programme will definitely continue. Offshoots such as cartoons are currently being developed. We took this up as a group project and our Platinum Group started seeing value in it. Given the turmoil communities have gone through in recent times, Makarapa City has been a good platform to tailor stories around their specific issues — including layoffs and unrest.

"We're working hard to listen to the conversations going on and giving communities what they want. The business units feed back to us on a day-to-day basis, so we can keep the programmes current and authentic. Our next series has a story line around retrenchment. This is a big issue and we have to bring it into the story. The same goes for xenophobia – these are great educational opportunities," says Ramchander.

"We're also looking at a fun way of educating the community with the various radio DJs asking: 'How many of you know what your cellphone is made from? Where does the material come from?' This helps explain why mining is so important. It can also educate the youngsters, combining fun and education. We play with ideas all the time to raise awareness about our role and our initiatives and to build trust."

Anglo American is taking communication to new heights – reaching the people where they're at, not expecting them to seek the information out.

 **EXERCISE**

Name and discuss five different internal communication channels giving the merits and disadvantages of each.

CHAPTER 2

USING SOCIAL MEDIA FOR INTERNAL COMMS

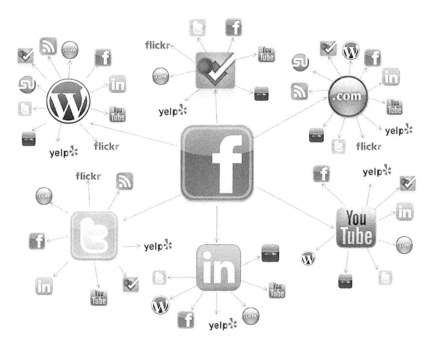

You know your staff, whether they're allowed or not, will most definitely be using social media whilst they're working. For most it's like breathing – they can't live without it. So why not harness this for the good of the company?

Most companies use internal communications for their public relations and marketing campaigns but shiver at the thought of using them for internal communications. They may use staff emailing and newsletters but anything more would be seen as letting staff chat online.

However more and more companies today are looking at the value of this form of reaching staff instantly and, more importantly, having their messages read. This is especially important today with people increasingly working remotely – individually or in teams.

SOCIAL MEDIA SECURITY

The biggest issue against communicating internally via social media is security leaks – for large organisations this includes sharing sensitive data or unfavourable personal opinions, for example.

An important part of using social media internally is to make staff realise the importance of their role as brand advocates. There are naturally problems that can occur here, in particular the exposure of private content through negligence, ignorance or other mistakes. This is where having confidentiality and social media policies in place and in contracts becomes essential.

Depending on the size of the organisation staff need to know from day one that the paragraphs around this issue in their contact aren't just words on paper, but could end up, if they abuse internal social media, with them losing their jobs.

When too much is too much

In 2012 Morgan Stanley, a financial services provider, decided they would let 17 000 financial advisors communicate through LinkedIn and Twitter with just one proviso – that they only release pre-written Tweets. The result was a dismal failure with very little notice taken of these generic messages.

The financial services sector is a perfect example where security concerns and fear of sensitive data being released have stopped companies using social media. At the same time this has affected their communications both internally and externally, leaving them behind other sectors.

Lack of trust is a difficult conundrum for organisations to get their heads around but heads have to be taken out of the sand and solutions found. Social media is here to stay and is the way people, including employees, communicate – so ways around these fears need to be found.

Why you should use social media within companies

One of the first companies to see the value of social media as an internal communications tool was Nokia, who in 2008 launched their BlogHub. This internal communication system allowed Nokia's employees to create their own internal community using posts, photos and videos.

It's not surprising when you hear that Nokia's motto is 'Connecting people and exploring ways to enhance communication'. Their initial aim was to: *"encourage the use of social media internally to bring out the company's unique authentic voice and engage in social media externally on behalf of Nokia and contributing to product and service announcements by opening up a dialogue and driving online engaging".*

According to Molly Schontal, who was part of the Social Media team in the USA, the BlogHub is Nokia's most powerful and effective internal social media tool. She explains:

> *"The BlogHub lowers barriers for employees to find conversations relevant to them. Rather than the company dictating a corporate culture and controlling how the line of internal comms should flow, the BlogHub allows employees to better understand messaging by communicating with people whose opinions matter. Everyone has a voice.*

> *"The BlogHub offers a dynamic community ruled by members, not executives," Schontal points out. Just by giving their input into blogs, posted ideas and knowledge are not only shared but awareness created around important issues – once again before they become toxic.*

> *Schontal adds, "In a massive company like Nokia, people can find out who inside this large organisation is doing something beneficial to them to make their jobs easier and likewise, which colleagues can benefit from their own knowledge and experience."*[1]

---

1   Schontal, M. 8 December 2015. Nokia's internal communication driven by social media. Simplycommunicate. Retrieved from: https://simply-communicate.com/nokias-internal-communication-driven-social-media/

Screenshot From Most Impressive Device in 2009?

Employee marketing

This is a new opportunity for companies to market their own ideas to staff, who will hopefully become enthusiastic about passing these on to potential customers. Studies have conclusively proven that employees who can post, Tweet and pin can still perform at peak levels – perhaps even more productively than those not allowed on social media. And the good news is that instead of hearing things through the company grapevine, internal company social media can be fully monitored.

Benefits of internal social networks

The fact they're going to be on social media, whether work related or not, for a great part of the day, means it's a short step to get them involved in social media marketing, making them instant social media company ambassadors.

Some bosses might say, 'but we send out company newsletters with all our news'. The answer to this is: 'but who really reads them?' Almost nobody. They end up buried under piles of paper on desks and often go straight into the bin or, if sent via intranet, simply get deleted before even being opened (see chapter five).

Knowing your staff spend a great deal of the day staring at their phone screens anyway means they're far more likely to see and read the latest news from HR or any other important company happenings.

The other exciting feature here is that you can also download short videos, which are becoming a vital part of communication these days. These could be videos of meetings or company events which could also be bookmarked for use later.

Again, looking at those employees who are either travelling or working remotely from outside the office, social media communication makes it easy for them to stay in touch with the latest company happenings.

Internal social media allows employees to:

- Celebrate their organisation

- Share company event news/photos/write-ups

- Share company achievements in real time

- Voice their opinions

- Share their ideas

- Easily connect with each other, locally, nationally or internationally

- Allows those who won't necessarily come forward in person to voice their views or concerns

Instant messaging

 There are again very few people who outside of the workplace don't use one or other of the ever-growing instant messaging apps, such as WhatsApp, on a daily basis. Whether organising a family get-together or offering support through a difficult time, groups of people can communicate with ease, without having to send individual messages.

This then is obviously a great way for employees to communicate internally, whether in their own teams, departments or branches, with those within their own office or outside.

Advantages of using instant messaging:

- Chats can be archived for later reference

- Instant connection and collaboration with groups of colleagues

- Manage multiple conversations at once

- No battling to get hold of people on the phone

Most popular messaging apps in SA:

- WhatsApp

- Mxit

- WeChat

Intranet

Intranet usage has come a long way since its inception in the nineties. Today many companies find there's a crossover between intranet and social media with external feeds from Twitter, Facebook and Instagram appearing as well as content produced by employees being shared on external social media – which, of course, can be a security problem. But, at the same time, many companies are beginning to see value in aligning their internal and external messages to not only engage with their staff more effectively but to create customer awareness.

The intranet is a great place for:

- An employee calendar – showing company highlights, picnics or deadlines

- Blogs and newsletters

- Videos, podcasts, infographics

- Staff interviews

- Interviews with industry leaders

- Sharing research

- Photos

- Company polls

- Feedback

- Encouraging staff through sharing content – blogs, articles, white papers or reports

Support or discussion forums

Discussion forums on your intranet is yet another way to gauge the mood of your organisation as well as giving your employees a great way of discussing important issues or just sharing what's on their mind. Again, it's a way for companies to track ongoing conversations and see where or when action needs to be taken.

Benefits of discussion forums:

- Can help generate content creation

- Offer staff support (tutorials)

- Keep topics going outside of regular newsletters

- Help with internal market research

- Create knowledge bases – especially useful for new staff

- Quick way to gauge staff reactions

- Platform for sharing photos and videos

- Target specific groups

- Quizzes and surveys, e.g. Did staff get anything out of training sessions?

 # CASE STUDY: NOKIA'S BLOGHUB

Driven by employees and not the executives, this blog allows for conversations at the grassroots level. Issues that had previously been confined to one department are now brought to the attention of other members of staff across the organisation.

Employees are able to comment on the posts, allowing for an exchange of knowledge and opinions. By giving staff their own outlet for creative thinking, Nokia is encouraging the workforce to create their own solutions to issues in house whilst also promoting communication across the company.

Nokia's internal communication driven by social media

In a technologically savvy company like Nokia, it's no surprise that they've been successfully implementing social media into their internal communications. The company's motto is connecting people and exploring ways to enhance communication. To realize that vision, Nokia uses a number of different vehicles for two-way and push/pull communications; social media plays a big part with fitting into that strategy. Nokia utilises social media in many of its divisions.

Nokia's Social Media Communications team was established in early 2008 with the aim of improving inter-company communications and engaging employees. The objective of the Nokia Social Media Communications team is to: encourage the use of social media internally to bring out the company's unique authentic voice and to engage in social media externally on behalf of Nokia, and contributing to product and service announcements by opening up a dialogue and driving online engagement.

CASE STUDY: STANDARD BANK'S YAMMER

Kate Johns, Head, Africa Communications, Standard Bank:

Use of social media in the workplace a growing trend given high levels of social media outside the work place. Comes with a great deal of work in ensuring that governance, compliance and permission legalities have been covered before implementing.

Kevin Welman, Director, ByDesign Communications:

Social media plays a critical role in society, including the workplace. Wars have started because of social media, governments have been overthrown, companies have been driven into the ground – in each instance there was a problem beforehand, social media simply emphasised the issues and built a community around that issue.

Social media has completely rewritten the rule book on news, on crisis management etc.

Solly Moeng, Managing Director and Senior Consultant, DonValley Brand, Marketing and Communications Agency:

Social media is here to stay and cannot be wished away. Reputation conscious organisations should have guidelines in place on what constitutes accepted conduct on social media, especially in regard to use during office hours and identification with and comments that involve the brand (corporate/product/service). The 'dos and don'ts' should be spelled-out clearly, underpinned by corporate values. Where corporate values do not exist, or have not been adequately communicated, people risk placing corporate reputation in peril through their conduct.

Daniel Munslow, CPRP, Independent Communication and Brand Consultant:

Social media is being used increasingly more strategically, but needs more change management support to influence the change. People use platforms for content more than anything else, so a good channel on its own isn't achieving anything. Also, as much as social media is important, organisations must not get tunnel-visioned into thinking this channel is the solution to all their issues. New Enterprise social media tools are becoming more important, but given the geographic diversity of our audiences, they must be used as one element of many other channels.

 **EXERCISE**

1. Show three different ways where social media would make a major impact on internal communications.

2. What would be the main issues to take into consideration before implementing a platform such as *Yammer*?

CHAPTER 3

EMAILS

From:

To:

I vividly remember my first attempt at using email. It was in the mid 1990s and I was sending a story through to *Men's Health* magazine's then deputy editor Jason Brown. There I was in Johannesburg on the phone to Jason in Cape Town who was valiantly trying to explain this complex procedure to me. My thoughts, which I verbalised to Jason were: "I'll never get this right..."

Emails changed all our lives. As a freelance journalist in particular my journey had gone from sending stories down to Cape Town from Johannesburg in the 'night bag' to the wonders of Fax and then email.

Emails have revolutionised the way business is done around the world, making communication quicker, easier and often more hazardous. Why hazardous? Simple – because with a letter, unless it was obviously junk mail, you would at least open it and glance at the contents before deciding what to do with it. In the case of business people they would generally have a secretary who would do it for them, reading each letter in case there was anything of consequence there. They would then present these to their bosses, pointing out anything of specific importance.

Today emails pop up on the screen, often every few seconds or minutes, and the tendency in our busy, overworked schedules is to glance at the heading and simply press delete, often before even bothering to open the email. And then you get that call asking what you thought of so and so's email that said… You instantly realise that was one you deleted and fumble your way through a conversation while frantically searching through your deleted items!

STYLES OF EMAIL COMMUNICATION

Conversational style

An email is more like a conversation than a formal letter or memo. But the way we speak and write is often quite different. In speech we pause, vary our tone, convey meaning through facial expressions and body language, as well as working out what the person listening to us is thinking. So the challenge is to strike a balance between conversational language and the written word – to ensure it's as clear when we write as when we speak.

And if your email is work related you still have to keep a professional image and tone. And remember, **be careful what you put in an email**, as it's often seen by people other than those you send it to.

Formal or informal

Most importantly, never use email as a shield to hide personal hostility or to send negative news you feel uncomfortable giving in person. If you receive an upsetting or insulting message don't respond immediately. Wait! Then decide on your tone by:

- Considering your relationship with the reader. Is it familiar, positive, friendly, tense, formal, business?

- Identifying the reader's likely point of view, needs, expectations, concerns, possible biases, attitudes and interests.

- Determining the main reason for your email. Does it have more than one purpose? Maybe separate emails would be the way to go.

- Understanding how much detail the reader needs (times, dates, examples, addresses, names) to avoid information overload.

- Asking if and how much the reader may care about the content of your email?

- Thinking about whether you would want to receive and read your own email?

You'll notice this book is written using more conversational language than formal – that's because it's easier for you to digest and hopefully remember. So, in an email you could write:

I'll call you if the package doesn't arrive by noon on Friday.

Rather than:

I shall call you if the package does not arrive by noon on Friday.

Clarity

How many times have you received an email and thought 'Huh – no idea what they want...' Here's an example of one I received recently together with my reply:

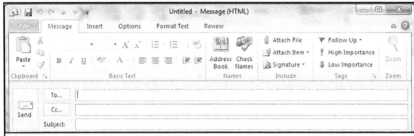

Hi Marion,

Hoping this finds you well and that things have been good.

I have a client that is showcasing some of their work in CT on the 16th of November. They are a satellite communications company. I wanted to pick your brain regarding possible colleagues that may want to attend to see if they can get published? It's very technical stuff but so interesting in terms of the capabilities.

Looking forward to hearing from you

Regards

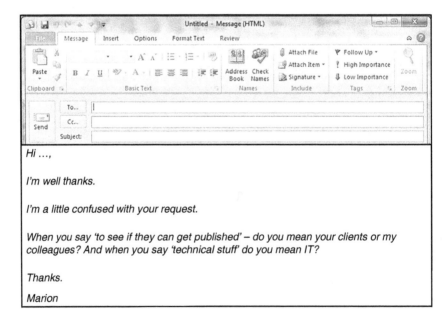

Hi ...,

I'm well thanks.

I'm a little confused with your request.

When you say 'to see if they can get published' – do you mean your clients or my colleagues? And when you say 'technical stuff' do you mean IT?

Thanks.

Marion

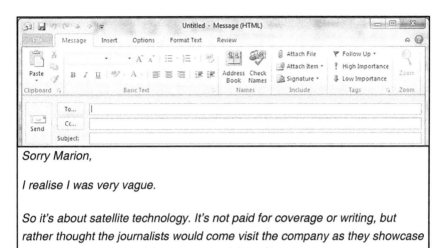

Sorry Marion,

I realise I was very vague.

So it's about satellite technology. It's not paid for coverage or writing, but rather thought the journalists would come visit the company as they showcase their products and see if they can get published?

Does this make more sense? The answer here was a resounding 'not really...'

EMAIL ETIQUETTE

Introductions

If you're not sure whether the person receiving your email knows you or remembers meeting you, just jog their memory on who you are.

> *Hi Tumi,*
>
> *It was really good to meet you at the conference last week...*

Or

> *Hi Joe,*
>
> *It was good of your colleague Bella to introduce us and as promised I'm sending you ...*

Tone

We spoke about tone in the previous chapter and this is particularly relevant in emails. Right from the opening you set the tone with your greeting. Remember, the person receiving it can't hear your voice or see your face. How would you take the following?

> *Joe,*
>
> *I need you to do....*
>
> *Hi Joe,*
>
> *Please could you do ...*

Or even worse, no greeting at all and straight into what you want. We are all guilty of leaving off the greeting at times – especially when we're going back and forth on an email conversation – but at the beginning of this conversation there's a need for a proper greeting.

Email bravado

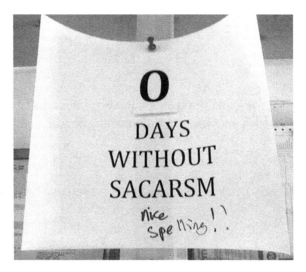

Email means you can hide behind your words. After all, writing a sarcastic message is a lot easier than saying it to someone's face. We've all had that moment when in sheer frustration we tap out a reply and before we know it, we've hit the send button – only to think twice immediately after. Rather wait – cool down and think out a measured reply.

Dear Sir, Dear Joe, Hi Joe or Hi?

There's no one-size-fits-all answer here. It totally depends on who you're writing to and the level of formality that goes with that. For instance, if you're writing to a company asking for a job then the 'Dear ....' would be expected as it would in any formal business situation.

Once you've got a relationship with someone or they're a peer of yours then 'Hi ...' is perfectly acceptable.

Just using someone's name however is never acceptable. It's almost as though you're trying to talk down to, shout at or even belittle the person, as in:

> *Marion,*
>
> *I received your email and need the following done immediately...*

Again it all comes down to tone.

Writing in capitals!

I had a client many years ago whose staff approached me with a pressing problem. Please could I speak to their boss and tell her to stop writing all her emails to them in capital letters. They felt she was shouting at them. And nine times out of ten she was. It's simply rude, and needless to say, she didn't win any popularity stakes with her staff. So use capital letters sparingly – not as a general rule. The same goes for exclamation marks – they have the same effect.

Spelling names correctly

This is essential and yes, it might take a few minutes to find this out but there's no shortcut when it comes to getting names right. It's saying to someone, 'I don't really care about you or how your name is spelt.'

This might be as easy as a Google search or you may have to call the person's office or home. The extra time is worth it. If you're talking to someone over the phone and they're spelling their name, then make sure you get each letter, as in 'M' for mother, 'E' for echo...

Don't assume because someone's name is John, it's not spelt Jon, or that Tumi isn't Thumi.

Grammar and spell check

Would you leave home in the morning without fixing your hair or thinking about your appearance? The answer is almost definitely no. And you probably wouldn't send off a document without using spell check first – well, don't send off an email without it either. You may not bother to check your spelling mistakes but the person receiving it will notice and their impression of you will match your bad spelling.

And don't forget good grammar. Spell check doesn't really take care of grammar and the only way you'll know whether your email makes sense is to read it aloud. This will also allow you to hear the tone you've used and whether you have this right.

Make sure you have used your apostrophes correctly and not overdone the !!!! or ??? These can be taken as rude or condescending.

Reason for the email

Assuming you're clear on why you're sending the email, will the person receiving it understand? Are you requesting information, confirming something, giving feedback? Make sure you have all the relevant details or information necessary to make your email effective. Stay away from generalities which can be confusing. You don't want the reader to read the mail twice to try and figure out what you want.

Attachments

If you're sending a large attachment then you might want to check what would be the best time or way to send this so you don't block the person's inbox, causing other mails to bounce. Or send multiple attachments over a few emails. There are many ways to send a large document, either through cloud storage such as Dropbox, file transfer or by compressing them.

Most importantly, never open an attachment from someone you don't know.

Reply to all

Don't use this unless each person you've listed is involved in this email, otherwise their inbox will be filled with unnecessary mails meant for your eyes.

Email forwarding

Be very careful when you're forwarding emails. Check that they don't contain any private or sensitive information. Internal mail in particular must stay just that – internal.

Most companies have a security policy that prohibits internal company data from being sent outside the company without proper security.

If this is part of a long email thread then rather summarise the discussion in your email than expect the person to wade through each message.

The dangers of SMS language used in emails

Whilst there's nothing wrong if you're texting a friend and using these acronyms, they definitely don't belong in the world of emails, especially in the business arena. In other words, type in complete sentences.

Checking addresses

Don't wait until the email comes back to you to check whether you're sending it to the right address or whether the email is a .com or .co. za… Check first.

Acknowledging emails

Just because someone doesn't ask for a reply doesn't mean they don't want one. Always answer emails from people you deal with promptly. A simple: 'Thanks, I'll look at this and get back to you,' will suffice. If they need an acknowledgement of a particular point, say to move on with a project, then make sure you give that assurance.

Alternatively if you're not happy with something in the email, then don't sit with it for a few days before voicing your feelings. Write back straight away saying what you feel and asking for other action to happen.

EXAMPLE

Acknowledging receipt of an order

Dear Mr ...

Thank you for your order of 100 chrome Rare Earth Magnets. We have these in stock and we're able to deliver to you within three days.

Unless otherwise instructed, we'll deliver these to your Midrand depot.

Do let us know if there's anything else we can do for you and once again we appreciate your giving us your business.

Kind regards,

Joe Soap
Sales Manager

Subject line

Generally, people spend milliseconds deciding whether to open your email – especially if they don't know you. The only thing between your email and the delete button is the subject line, so spend a while to see whether the subject matter actually reflects your email. If it doesn't instantly grab them, too late, you're history.

Short and sweet

Research shows subject lines with 30–50 characters or less result in 12% higher opening rates and 75% higher click-through rates. Don't waste space on unnecessary words. Go through it carefully to see what you can take out, without losing the meaning. A good example here are the words, *the* and *that*, eg: 'The delivery that you are waiting for': 'The delivery you are waiting for'. Or, even better, use a contraction as in: 'The delivery you're waiting for'.

And never put anything in the subject line that can go in the body of the email.

Catch their attention and don't mislead

Not everyone can write catchy lines so don't overtry on this. Rather write a straightforward heading that accurately relates what you're writing about as in:

Response to your query on delivery

Or

Invitation to launch of new Volvo

One email – one request

How many times have you sent an email asking someone more than one thing to find they only come back to you answering the first thing you asked for? A quick easy tip here is this:

- One request per email
- Three requests – three emails

This way you'll get all your answers.

Length of email

Ask a busy person how many emails they get in a day and you'll probably find it's a good few hundred. So bear this in mind when you're writing your email and spare some thought for the person who has to read it.

Although there's no rule on what's the exact length of a good email, always try to be as brief and concise as you can, sticking to the subject you gave in the subject line. If you need a long conversation, pick up the phone.

Don't give your whole life story in the first paragraph or where you found the person's email address – just get straight to it. Stick to the tried and tested five w's and an h: what, where, why, when, who and how. Well, maybe not quite like that – but stick to the facts of why you're writing. Don't bury the message somewhere at the end where it's likely to be missed completely.

Clarity

Know what you expect from the person you're writing to and make sure this comes across in the first two sentences of your email. Don't build up to the big question or point. Do you want to meet this person? Do you want them to send you something? Do you need information? Be polite and get to the point as quickly as possible.

Conclusions

Always end your emails with 'Thank you', 'Sincerely', 'Best regards' – anything friendly but definitely something.

When to send your email

Is there really an optimum time to send an email? Absolutely. Think about someone's day and work out when they're most likely to read their mails. Early morning? Late at night? If you don't get a response after trying both, then try a completely different time of day.

EMAIL FORMAT

- The same goes for using bold as caps – be careful how you use it.

- Don't use patterned backgrounds or multiple colours which make the email harder to read.

- Use plain fonts. Most emails are set at Calibri 11 but you could use Arial or Times New Roman and black is the safest choice.

- Stay away from emoticons – unless you're writing to family or friends.

- Don't type your emails all in lower case which really looks lazy.

Email signature

Whilst it's important to look professional don't overdo it…

Out of office replies

This is a polite way of stopping people wondering why they haven't received a reply from you and when you'll be back in the office. If you can give an alternative name and address/number of a person to contact, that could help them if the matter is urgent.

Sending emails from your phone

The dangers of predictive text

A man texts his neighbour:

> *I'm sorry. I've been riddled with guilt and I have to confess. I have been helping myself to your wife when you're not around, probably more than you.*

> *I know it's no excuse but I don't get it at home. I can't live with the guilt any longer. I hope you'll accept my sincerest apology. It won't happen again.*

The man, feeling outraged and betrayed, grabs his gun, goes into the bedroom and without a word shoots his wife.

Minutes later he gets a second text:

> *I really should use spell check! That should be 'wifi'... Sorry!*

We've all done this – well, maybe not to this degree – but unless you read through your email or message texts you could find yourself in hot water. Or, at the very least, thought of as downright dumb because you don't make any sense. Just like anything else, when you send emails or text messages don't forget to read them through – aloud.

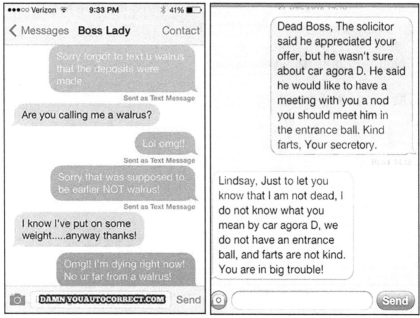

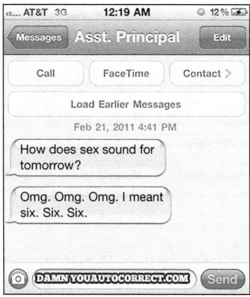

Email considerations

- Before assuming someone hasn't responded, always check your trash or junk folder.

- Never send off an emotionally charged email at once – rather wait a day.

- If an email chain has been running check the subject matter is still relevant – otherwise change it.

- Make sure you read your email out loud to check for mistakes and whether it reads well.

- Don't reply to old emails when you're writing about a totally new topic.

- Check your virus programme is up to date.

CASE STUDY

Helen White, Director of Communications and Fundraising, ORBIS Africa (Eye Health Care NGO):

As a global organisation we have to take into account different styles in email communications. The United States will immediately get down to business, so there's no 'Dear Helen, Hope you're well.' It will almost go straight into bullet points. So you can't get offended – it's just their style.

Our CEO will often send out a global message to around 40 recipients, most of whom will press 'reply all' when they respond, which can be really annoying. If for instance it's an email about a new appointment you will receive all the emails welcoming the person to the team and telling them how glad you are they're here! We need to keep emails to the bare minimum and to the point.

Often it's so much easier to pick up the phone, especially when you're talking to multiple countries. We use Zoom, (a cloud video conferencing service) a lot which saves on airfares straight away.

Emails should be sent prior to discussions to cut through the clutter. They shouldn't always be the first point of call. After a Zoom or Joinme call you can use email to follow up.

If you find there's a chain of emails on a particular topic remember to change the subject headings as the discussion changes. Your topic may have shifted or been updated and people lose focus as to what the conversation is now about. This also helps for record keeping and tracking purposes.

I find it unacceptable to find spelling errors in emails when it's easy to put Spellcheck as an automatic setting in your emails. Perhaps it's because people are now using Smartphones and tablets to send emails they have become so informal they feel it's ok to have typos and be less professional. An email from a phone should be as correct as one from a computer. And that means no emojis and smiley faces...

The biggest problem with emails according to:

Solly Moeng, Managing Director and Senior Consultant, DonValley Brand, Marketing & Communications Agency:

The biggest problem is language use. Many communicators, especially juniors, still confuse spoken language with written language. They also lack the understanding to use the right tone for the right addressee.

Another problem is the assumption many seem to make, which consists of sending important/urgent information by email and failing to follow-up with a telephone call to ensure the information has been received by the intended recipient. This often results in deadlines being missed and organisations either missing-out on opportunities or incurring unnecessary fines.

Finally, failure to ensure that what gets written in the subject line corresponds with the content of the email. This can be confusing, at best, and irritating, at worst. It's always important to remember adjusting the subject line as discussions develop, where this is necessary.

Kevin Welman, Director, ByDesign Communications:

The challenge with email is that it's a transaction – an impersonal technology based transaction. Good communicators realise this and know when to email; when you're sharing or capturing information, but if you want interaction with the aim of solving a problem people should be speaking to each other. Email has made it too easy to hide from your responsibilities or from the relationships you need to establish and cultivate.

Kate Johns, Head, Africa Communications at Standard Bank:

A complete over reliance on email everywhere! Tone and nous are the two major problems I see with email as it's difficult to gauge either/both in the written form. But that said, more and more journalists make initial contact with me by email rather than the telephone.

Daniel Munslow, CPRP, Independent Communication and Brand Consultant:

Email is a challenge due to overload and the superficial nature of the content it contains. As a result, when there is something strategic, it's generally overlooked. Email is not segmented properly, thereby confusing the messages that are landing with stakeholders but sharing generic and often useless information to the people that actually receive it.

It's a complex exercise of engaging IT and HR to ensure databases are correct and accurately segmented to ensure relevance of message. Therefore, relevance, segmentation, accuracy of content, and volume of information overload are the key issues. Further, there is no two way communication with email.

 **EXERCISE**

You are setting guidelines for your company on emails. Lay out your rules and clearly indicate which types of correspondence these refer to.

CHAPTER 4

FORMS OF COMMUNICATION

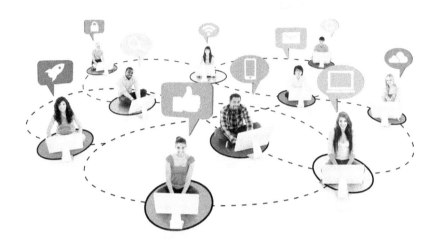

LETTERS

We've certainly come a long way from writing on tablets but even so you may look at this and think – letters, who sends those anymore? And to a degree you would be right. We very rarely, if ever, actually 'type' a letter, print it out, put it into an actual envelope and post it. Why would we, when at the touch of a button an email will reach its destination instantly, together with any documents, music, even photos and videos. The question remains: is an email the same as a letter – just in a different format?

Key to writing a good letter is knowing and understanding who you're writing to. If you're writing to a friend as opposed a colleague or the CEO of a large corporation, you'll craft the letter in a specific style. If you understand this you're half way to becoming a good correspondent.

When is a letter necessary?

Personal letter

Sometimes a handwritten note is the only way to go and will earn you great kudos with the person receiving it. Maybe you're thanking them for some thoughtful thing they did for you or letting them know you're thinking of them.

Formal letters

To,

The Manager
ABC Ltd.

Sub: Thank you for job offer

Dear Sir,

This is with reference to the job offer letter that I have received from ABC Limited (Date:___) for the post of Marketing Manager. I would like to thank you for your job offer to work at ABC Ltd. After our interview, I only became more eager at the prospect of joining your marketing team. I understand and accept all the terms in this offer. I shall complete all the obligatory formalities before the contract is signed. In addition, I will also submit all the necessary documents prior to the joining date.

Please keep me updated on any information you deem pertinent. You have all my contact information, but the best way to reach me is through my e-mail address.

Again, thank you so much for the opportunity. I am excited to work on such a meaningful project, and I look forward to working in such a creative environment.

Sincerely,

Loyds Kimble

Interestingly enough, when looking at the birth of emails, they certainly didn't look as they do today. They were far more like traditional letters. Email writing has evolved over time – not always to the betterment of communications.

The biggest difference between letters and emails today is the speed and shortness of the letter. But this doesn't take away from certain situations where the more formal style is definitely needed.

One problem with emails as opposed to letters arriving through the post, is that people would always open their post, even if they then discarded a particular letter. Many emails get deleted before they have even been opened...

The longer emails are around, the worse, it seems, becomes the content and in the business world this just won't cut it.

For instance, receiving something like this:

Hi,

I c you are looking for someone to do communication i can definately (sic) do that. can i come and c u?

Joe

The answer quite obviously is NO, involving a primal scream at the same time.

In other words you can't write a casual email the same way you would write a formal business letter, certainly not one applying for a position.

In fact, whether you're writing an email or a letter you shouldn't be using the same language (as in 'c u' and r) that you use in sms language.

Parts of a Letter

Contact information

A letter, as against an email, will generally be on a letterhead with all the contact information at the top, as opposed to an email with this at the end.

Date

We don't date emails as the date automatically appears, but in the context of a formal letter the date should be there.

Address

This again is only applicable to a business letter and should give the name of the person you're writing to, their title and company name. If you don't have a name, just a position, then write, 'Head of IT'.

Greetings

This is perhaps the biggest factor that differentiates emails from letters, although even in a business-related email there should be times you don't start with 'Hi...', but rather 'Dear Ms....'

A letter generally starts with 'Dear...' This can be 'Mr, Mrs or Ms...' Or, if you feel you can use their first name, then 'Dear Grace' will do. The best way of judging this is to look at their correspondence to you, if there is any, and see what format they use. If they've written 'Hi...' then the door's open for you to do the same.

Body of letter

This can be one paragraph or several, depending on the purpose of the letter – which is the key factor here. Why are you writing this at all? Letters generally start with an introductory paragraph and a short explanation of why you're writing. Following on from this, there should be one or possibly two paragraphs going into just enough detail so the reader understands what you expect from them.

Closing

The final paragraph would either request some kind of action from the reader or consist of a final comment that ties up the first few paragraphs.

 EXAMPLE

Dear Mr Sibanda,

Thank you for your quote to carry out the building work on our new premises. Whilst you have covered all the areas we highlighted in our meeting with you last month, there have recently been some new developments on the project.

Before giving you a final answer on your quote could you please let us have the following costs:

- Replacing the tiled patio with a wooden deck

- Changing the window frames from wood to aluminium

- Adding awnings to the outside patios

Obviously you would need to visit our premises once again and Jackie is waiting for your call to set this up.

We're sorry this has taken so long but we need our offices to match our brand, which simply means being the best we can be. Looking forward to hearing from you soon.

Yours sincerely,

Signature

A signature at the end of a letter also differentiates an email from a formal letter. Before emails, letters would be dictated to a secretary who would type them up and return them for your signature. Whilst you may personally want to sign your letter, it's much more common to simply set up a permanent email signature which does away with having to print out the letter, sign it and then have to scan it back to the computer.

The look

CASSANDRA CARLISLE

3325 Ramon Road • San Francisco, California 94124
Phone: (415) 555-1212 • Email: support@resumeedge.com

March 19, 2002

Mr. Robert Simmons
Director of Human Relations
Stein, Field & Clairmont
111 Nob Hill Drive
San Francisco, California 94124

Dear Mr. Simmons:

This letter is to express my interest in joining your firm's Tax Department as an Associate. With a solid background in taxation, coupled with four academic degrees and current attendance in the Taxation Program at Stanford University's Law Center, I know I can make a positive contribution to your firm.

Briefly, my qualifications include:

- More than four years as a tax agent for Israel's Internal Revenue Service.
- Licensure in the State of Israel as a Certified Public Accountant.
- Successful completion of a legal internship under the supervision of the Deputy Chief Counsel of Israel's Internal Revenue Service.
- Work as an associate in the Tax Department of Mukdar, Neiman & Schwartz Co., one of Israel's most prestigious law firms specializing in commercial law and taxation.
- Expertise in tax law, including income, capital gains, and land betterment.
- An interest in international and US tax law.
- A B.A. in Accounting, an MBA in Finance and Accounting, an LL.B. (Juris Doctorate equivalent), and an LL.M. in Commercial Law graduating magna cum laude in each from Tel Aviv University.
- LL.M. Candidacy in Stanford University Law Center's Taxation Program with an expected graduation date this May.

Additional qualifications can be found in the enclosed résumé and academic transcript.

In an effort to discuss this matter further, I will be calling your office within the next few days to see if we might set up a time to meet.

If you have any questions, I can be reached at the number above. Thank you for your attention.

Sincerely,

Cassandra Carlisle

Encl.

A formal business letter, even though in the format of an email, should still look professional, with plenty of space between paragraphs and the top and bottom of the page. This means choosing a readable font, such as Times New Roman 10 or Aerial 10.

Proofread and spell check

Lastly, make sure before you hit the send button that you have read it through – preferably out loud as you won't pick up mistakes by reading just with your eyes. You may notice mistakes you didn't catch the first time

And, of course, do a spell check and grammar check.

Memo

To: John Smith, Department Head

From: Jane Summers, CEO

Date: 19th May 2014

Subject: New Creative Strategy

MEMOS

Once again emails have taken the place of another common form of business communication – the memo. Previously, when a company wanted to communicate with members of staff internally, they used the memorandum – the memo. This would be typed, signed, printed and sent out around the office or pinned to the notice board next to the coffee corner, where everyone would see it.

So the question is whether the memo is still relevant?

The difference between an email and a memo

An email is a quick communication for someone to get information, possibly act on it and then delete. They're fast and generally efficient. The biggest difference between this and a memo is that a memo is more of a call to action for a purpose. It could be:

- A detailed proposal

- An important report

- A serious recommendation

- A technical explanation

- Minutes of a meeting

- A new policy

- Details of an upcoming compulsory event

One of the benefits of using a memo is that it allows you to use columns, tables, a graph, plenty of white space and even to convert the memo to a PDF, attached to an email. Another benefit is that a memo can be easily filed to refer to when you need it.

Memo Format

Sample of memo to staff

Generally printed on company letterhead.

 EXAMPLE

To: *All Staff*

From: *Samantha Manda, Personal Assistant to the CEO*

Date: *October 10th, 2017*

Subject: *Parking*

We have received numerous complaints around misuse of the parking area recently. These include:

- *Not parking within the white lines which means less space for anyone else*

- *Parking motorbikes in bays designated for cars*

- *Leaving cars overnight without permission*

We would really appreciate your cooperation here as we have limited space and want everyone to be able to park their cars safely.

Thanks.

Samantha Manda

Sample to customers

 **EXAMPLE**

To: *Customers of Introtel*

From: *Joe Soap, Public Relations Liaison*

Date: *October 10th, 2017*

Subject: *Change in invoicing*

In order to give you, our customer, optimum service, Introtel is introducing new accounting systems which will be in place by the end of next month. There are various factors for this change but above all we want you to know it's our commitment to excellence that once again drives this move.

We need to inform you this may entail slight problems with your accounts should they not be up to date and we would urge you to contact our accounts department if you have any queries around this.

The person to contact either during the change or after is:

Craig Washington – email: craigw@introtel.com – 069 698 7777

We're sorry if this inconveniences you in any way but we know the new system will make it even easier for you to do business with us.

Best,

Joe Soap

NOTICES

Again, the question – why a notice? Why not an email or a memo? A notice is a far more public notification which is often pinned up or stuck on a board where the people you want to reach will see it. For instance in a school, university or on any notice board – community or private – to announce events, celebrations or possibly sales. In other words where you wouldn't have a list of email addresses but need to communicate a message to a large number of people.

Government departments, parastatals or large organisations often use notices to publicise changes in legislation or even available jobs, which are generally published in newspapers.

Another instance is where an organisation has to reach a vast audience in a short space of time, for example, after the Ford Kuga debacle in January 2017 where eventually Ford had to recall certain Kuga models. This notice was published in major publications across the country:

> **PRETORIA, South Africa, January 16, 2017** – *Ford South Africa is issuing a safety recall for Kuga models equipped with the 1.6-litre engine to address an engine overheating condition that could cause a fire.*
>
> *A total of 4,556 vehicles are affected by this safety recall in South Africa, and were built between December, 2012 and February, 2014. Ford Kuga models with 1.5-litre and 2.0-litre engines are not affected.*

We have investigated the incidents as they have been reported to us, removing many parts for detailed examination in our engineering facilities in Europe and North America. The data collected from the recent incidents and the maintenance checks we are conducting through our dealers have helped us to determine the root cause of the fires.

While we continue to investigate the Kuga 1.6 engine compartment fires, based on the current data we have determined that the fires are due to engine overheating. This is caused by a lack of coolant circulation which can lead to a cracking in the cylinder head and, therefore, an oil leak. If the leaking oil reaches a hot engine surface, it can potentially catch fire. We are not aware of any injuries resulting from engine compartment fires.

With this safety recall, all affected vehicles, including those that have already been checked, must be taken to a Ford dealership as soon as possible. This safety recall comprises two stages.

The first stage involves replacing affected components on the cooling system, verifying and updating the software, and conducting an oil leak check on the cylinder head.

If any Kuga 1.6 owner sees any indication that the engine may be overheating or experiences warnings on the instrument cluster, they should pull over as soon as it is safe to do so, switch off the engine and ensure all occupants are safely out of the vehicle. For safety reasons, the bonnet must not be opened.

The emergency services should be called first, if required, then Ford's Roadside Assistance on 0861 150 250. Supported through the AA, this service is available 24/7.

The 1.6 Kuga is safe to drive, provided the integrity of the cooling system is maintained, and this safety recall has been actioned.

The next stage of the safety recall will make the cooling system even more robust, and is likely to involve further changes to parts and warning systems. We are currently ensuring that the changes we make are complete and thoroughly tested – and will communicate with our customers as soon as this stage commences.

Every effort is being made to minimize inconvenience, and reassure customers that their safety is our top priority.

We are committed to keeping our customers mobile. Should a customer experience any engine overheating problem with their 1.6 Kuga, or delays in the repair due to a shortage of parts, arrangements will be made through the nearest Ford dealer and Ford Customer Service to provide a courtesy car while the vehicle is repaired.

Any customer concerns or queries can be directed to Ford Customer Service at 0860 011 022.

Smaller notices

These could be for something as simple as asking staff to donate toys for a charity drive:

TOY DRIVE

On Friday 20th October Head Office will be donating toys to Cotlands Early Childhood Development Organisation Toy Library. If anyone would like to donate toys or books to this cause the details are given below:

Final Donation Date: Wednesday 18th October

Where to leave toys/books: In the collection boxes by reception

Types of toys: Preferably for ages 2 – 6

Many thanks.

Communications Department

They can also be used to advertise an internal position coming available:

Senior Accountant for Export Division

A senior accountant position will be available from 1st December, 2017 in our Export Division based in Cape Town. This division handles all fresh and frozen fruit exports to Europe and the United States.

The position requires providing financial information to management by researching and analysing accounting data; preparing reports.

Accountant Job Duties:

- Prepares asset, liability, and capital account entries by compiling and analysing account information

- Documents financial transactions by entering account information

- Recommends financial actions by analysing accounting options

- Summarises current financial status by collecting information; preparing balance sheet, profit and loss statement, and other reports

- Substantiates financial transactions by auditing documents

- Maintains accounting controls by preparing and recommending policies and procedures

- Guides accounting clerical staff by coordinating activities and answering questions

- Reconciles financial discrepancies by collecting and analysing account information

- Secures financial information by completing database backups

For more information contact: ....

 **EXERCISE**

Your company has been taken over by a large conglomerate and you want your loyal customers to know that your staff will remain intact and your services as good as ever.

- Write a letter to your customers with this news.

- Write a memo to your staff reassuring them of their jobs and encouraging them to carry on as always...

CHAPTER 5

NEWSLETTERS

Okay, admit it – how many of you actually read your internal newsletters? If my research is correct then the answer is very few. At one time internal newsletters came in one format – print, followed by both print and online. Today many companies have done away with print altogether and are just using online which brings us to the big question:

Online or Hard Copy?

If you don't already have a newsletter in place then whether to go online/intranet or print a hard copy is generally the hardest decision. If you only have hard copy this is an issue you have to look at.

Advantages of online

- Low cost. No printing costs or pain of distribution, plus you are being eco-friendly and saving paper!
- Reach the audience immediately

Disadvantages of online

- The delete button
- Not always taken as seriously as a hard-copy tangible one
- Articles have to be even shorter than hard copy as people don't read online – they scan!
- Pics have to be high resolution if they are to look good

Advantages of hard copy

- They can either be kept on the desk and read in between other work or
- Taken home and read at leisure – in taxis, planes or even in the loo…
- Kept for reference purposes
- Used to show prospective employees/shareholders about your business
- Often read by clients to get a better feel of the business

Disadvantages of hard copy

- Can easily be popped into the dustbin
- Can just get buried under mounds of other paper
- Simply not read…

Either way, the crucial element here is to get your staff to read what's happening within your organisation. This isn't always easy, especially in an organisation where you have different levels of readers from blue-collar workers right through to executives to be catered for. So the most important aspect here is giving your staff what THEY want – not what *you* think they should read.

What Staff Want

The most important issue when putting together any in-house magazine or newsletter is to be proactive, making sure you know your reader and what they want. How do you do this? If you're starting from scratch or already have an existing newsletter it's easy – ask them. If you have an existing newsletter ask them what they like, dislike or give them some ideas and see which boxes they tick. For example:

- Hatched, matched and despatched news

- Sporting event news (team results and pics)

- New staff members

- Bios on existing staff members

- News from departments

- Latest company advertising campaign news

- Sales news

- Social news and pictures

- Health issues

- How-to articles

- Humour

- Calendar of upcoming events

- Crosswords

- Sudoku

These are just some examples of content your staff may be interested in. You could also ask them to tell you what they're not interested in. Probably the message from HR or financial director!

Articles like the message from the MD or chairman are inevitable but we'll touch on that later.

Keep it new AND newsy!

There's absolutely no point in wasting time telling staff news they already know, so be aware of only printing new news!

Make sure staff know you're always looking for interesting stories. Maybe some staff are involved in great volunteer work and deserve a pat on the back or maybe you have a few good humour writers out there. And you can (legally) take certain stuff off the internet – with appropriate credits – and use that to spice up blank pages.

Most companies include a hatched, matched and despatched, but this depends on the size of your organisation. If your organisation has a staff of hundreds or even thousands, then do you care that Josie from sales is getting married to her childhood sweetheart Clint? Or that Thami from HR had a bouncing baby boy, who looks just like his mother? For small companies this is good because everyone knows who they're reading about. Otherwise it's generally a waste of space.

On the other hand, if a staff member is retiring after a long career in the company or has received a long-service award, this should be recognised, as should any awards received by staff members.

Style and tone

If it doesn't immediately grab the reader it'll either be deleted or go straight to File 13 – the dustbin. For staff to take the trouble to read your newsletter you must take the trouble to put together a professional, well laid out, *easily readable* publication.

In terms of style there's absolutely no reason an internal newsletter shouldn't be written in conversational style. It's supposed to be a chatty document so don't make it sound like a company report. The golden rule here is **WRITE AS YOU TALK!**

And remember, style isn't stagnant – it changes and so must your writing.

If someone starts telling you a story and uses boring 'old fashioned' language your mind starts to wander. You think: 'why don't they get to the point and quickly?' In other words whole forests are being sacrificed on the altar of waste paper.

We all have an elderly relative who will either tell you the same story over and over again or, even worse, tell a story in such minute detail that you're bursting to hurry them along. Don't let your readers feel the same.

It's all about reaching your audience, whether it's someone at the other end of your email or the reader of your website or publication.

Write as you speak

For some reason certain writers become Jane Austen when they stop speaking and start writing – DON'T. When your reader picks up your story they are engaging in a one-sided conversation with you speaking and them listening. Depending on your newsletter's style this can vary but you should never, for instance, use a word in prose that you wouldn't use in speech. For instance, do you use the word 'one' or 'boast', as in "My new car's really cool – it boasts a great sound system." – I don't think so... Or "One would think the Springboks would stand a good chance in the World Cup" – or not...

Layout and design

In terms of layout and design, if you have the budget then don't think twice about using a professional designer – at least to get your first issue/

re-issue off the ground. Learn how to design your newsletter so it looks fresh, crisp and appealing. Then don't forget to change it sometimes – don't let it become predictable – mix things up now and again.

GOOD EXAMPLE

BAD EXAMPLE – UNAPPEALING

White space

Avoid clutter and make sure there's plenty of white space. Rather use one or more extra pages than squash everything together over a few pages. Nothing puts people off more than pages full of heavy text. This is especially important with online publications. As people today are reading more online than off, the tendency is to scan a page, so pictures/graphics are even more important here.

SHORT AND SWEET

Story length

No story should be 'stretched' to fit the page. When you've got your story, you've got your story. Rather use an extra pic or graphic than fill the page with fluff for the sake of it. On the other hand, if you need a few extra words to really get home the crux of your story then beg for more – but not too often. And remember, less is more – but we'll look at this in editing. And remember, it's ok to add humour to some articles.

Treat your readers like children and remember they prefer pictures to words! No newsletter article should really be more than 350 words – less is even better. Nobody likes clutter – so break the articles/news into bite-size pieces.

In fact a photo or illustration with a caption is more likely to be read than most articles. If other people are contributing to your newsletter, especially experts in specific technical or academic fields, then issue a standard editorial brief such as:

- Use conversational style – using contractions, such as 'can't', 'wouldn't' etc.
- No article to be more than 300/350 words
- Avoid company jargon – in case this is read outside the company
- Remember to keep the reader's interest
- Don't use a long word when a short, simple one will do
- Write to express – not impress with how extensive your vocabulary is
- When using technical/academic language please include a box with explanations
- Use illustrations, photos, diagrams where possible

CONTENT

Getting the message across

When you're the one writing the article the first step is to put yourself in the shoes of your audience. What do they need to know and want to hear? What will stop them listening to what you have to say? And how will you know they have got the message?

Ask yourself the following – are you trying to:

- Provide new information?
- Explain a new product or service?
- Review a new product or service?
- Introduce a member of staff?
- Open up debate on an issue?
- Explain or justify decisions and actions?
- Motivate a reader to decide or act?
- Persuade the reader to understand or accept your viewpoint or position?
- Push a particular idea?

Most importantly, combined with any of the above, a newsletter should be entertaining – no matter how serious the subject matter, the reader has to be entertained to keep on reading.

BUT there are only so many stories and so many ways of telling them. That sounds logical, but to get people's attention in the digital world we live in we have to find new ways of writing the same stories. The point being to **TELL YOUR READERS SOMETHING THEY DON'T ALREADY KNOW.**

When your writing is centred around one organisation and industry, this can be particularly difficult. After all, there are only so many ways you can describe a new machine for cutting wood – no matter which way you write it. So how do you come up with new angles on the same themes? A good place to start is teamwork. Try, when possible, to bounce ideas off other members of your comms team – you'll be surprised what two or five heads come up with. Working as a team you'll often find new ways to approach regular features and news stories and find new sources for stories. Tap into international sites on similar topics and get ideas – obviously don't cut and paste, but there's nothing wrong with finding different ways of looking at topics.

Then, of course, there's the tried and tested method of journalism – network; keep your eyes and ears open. Attend as many work-related conferences and seminars as you can and mix with key players in your industry. You'll make contacts and maybe get the 'hot story' before anyone else.

Lastly, read the newspapers every day and pick up on what's news now. Take a news story and find an angle for your readers:

- If school or university fees are an issue, research options on how to either save for this or find bursary opportunities.

- If a survey shows that South Africans are the unhealthiest eaters in the world, then research ways of encouraging your staff to eat healthily and exercise more. Maybe encourage staff to start support groups and fitness clubs.

Researching your story

If you're writing about a company project that's happening reasonably close by, then get in your car, take your camera and go and see exactly what's happening. Only by speaking to the people involved and those affected by the project will you really understand what's going on and write a meaningful story.

So often in company newsletters the content comes from notices or factual accounts of an event. Nobody cares that much what a project costs, they're far more interested in the effect the project had on people.

Social Responsibility Programmes

Let's say your projects for the year include sponsoring an early childhood learning development programme, which involves a number of informal crèches in a poor community. You're given a document that lists the names of these crèches, where they're situated, how many children attend and how the owners are being helped by your company. You could simply print this but why not look at how you could make this more interesting?

Step One

Find out who you need to talk to and set up a visit, making sure the people concerned are there to guide you and show you exactly what they're doing.

Step Two

Try to organise your visit so you get the full experience of the children's day. Get there early and capture the excitement of the beginning of their school day, break and nap time, lessons and lunchtime. You can't do this from reading a piece of paper – you have to experience it, hear the children's laughter and see them hugging their teachers as they say goodbye for the day.

Step Three

Make sure you take lots of photos. You don't necessarily need an expensive camera – these days most phones will take quality shots, although you would have to check what kind of resolution you need. With this type of story, photos are vital. Words can never do justice to the joy on a child's face when they rush out to play with a friend or the intensity of listening to a well-read story.

Step Four

Write a story around your photos, using quotes from teachers, crèche owner, parents and, of course, the children. Make your company proud to be part of this project.

The scourge of cut and paste

In the digital age, gathering information on anything from nuclear physics to the latest movies is within the touch of a Google click. And it's just as easy to do the dreaded cut and paste. But there are several issues that arise from this. Is it ethical? Is it original? How soon before your readers get tired of this type of information?

This doesn't mean you can't use the net to find interesting short snippets for your readers around issues they would find interesting. What it does mean is that you shouldn't steal whole articles and publish them under your company's banner. There is such a thing as the law of copyright, linked to a dirty word – plagiarism!

Rather take the idea from the story and make it your own. Ask some staff members questions around the topic and even feature their photo with their comments.

 EXAMPLE

 You see a piece on bullying in the workplace, where a psychologist has been interviewed, plus some people who have experienced this. Why not do the same and make it your own? If you don't know a psychologist to interview ask your HR department if they know any or contact an organisation such as SADAG (The South African Depression and Anxiety Group) and ask them for the name of a specialist in this field. They would probably also have case studies for you.

Finding people in your own company to talk to you on their bullying experiences might be a little trickier, but by promising anonymity you might well find some. How? By Facebooking colleagues, keeping your ears open and asking around.

Interviewing skills

Often, when you want to interview a specific person, especially a busy one or just someone who doesn't want to be interviewed, you have to have patience. Be prepared to explain exactly why you want to interview them and the benefit your readers will get from the interview.

Try and choose a place to do the interview that's not noisy – i.e., not your staff canteen or a coffee shop. Preferably in the person's office where there's no external noise. Whilst you're in their office take note of what photos are on the desk (do they have kids?), what awards are on their wall – these details tell you so much about the person.

Most importantly, make sure you've done your homework before you arrive for your interview. At the very least, get their CV. And Google them – you never know what you might find!

Be confident, even if it's your CEO or a member of the board. Never be overawed or intimidated by your interviewee.

If you haven't managed to get quite enough background information, then try asking questions that will draw out answers such as:

Instead of:

Do you think the effect of last year's strikes in our industry is still affecting us?

Ask:

Tell us how last year's strikes still affect us today.

Equipment

Your mobile phone. Most have a recording device or you can download a recording app (available at reasonable prices and which are really easy to operate). By recording the interview rather than taking notes you're sure not to miss a single word. Then make sure you keep the interview until it's published just to cover your tracks.

Interview questions

Number one rule: Consider your readership

What do they want to know about your subject? Remember, once you've shaken hands and said goodbye it's really hard to go back and ask more questions, and your story is only going to be as good as your interview.

Have a list of questions ready **but** try not to look down every two minutes. This is also off-putting for your interviewee. A good interviewee will probably answer most of your questions without you even asking.

Remember the jargon rule – don't let them talk in language even you don't understand, never mind your readers. Also bear in mind your staff wants to get to know the real person behind the title. Try and get them to give you some personal information. Get them to relax and talk about their family or hobbies. For instance, if they like jazz, try and find out where they go to listen and what they drink while they're listening...

Remember, when you're writing the piece you need to keep your reader's attention and the little human points that come out make the story more interesting. We all like to know people's foibles and strange habits. It also helps to provide you with useful links for your story. Think of these as the colour parts of your story.

Above all, listen carefully and don't interrupt. You may interrupt their flow in such a way that they don't remember where they were – and you may just miss a gem of a comment.

What often works well in internal newsletters and helps staff see a different side of people is the question-and-answer type of interview.

EXAMPLE

A COMPANY Q & A

1. **What makes you want to come to work each day?**

   The challenge and excitement of growth, of problem-solving, of adapting to a changing world and the joy of working with and leading so many special people who are as passionate about this business as I am.

2. **How long have you been at xxxxxx?**

   20 years, excluding a two-year break where I left to start a small business in the fashion rag trade – which was great fun but with which I got bored quite quickly. I was recruited back to xxxxx in July 2005, just after the merger of the Home Care and Personal Care businesses, with the brief to help transform the company to a fast and flexible, high-growth, united business. In 2014 I went on secondment and spent just over two years working in the Global Category in the UK and I've been back since 2016, in our wonderful business and country.

3. **How many departments/functions have you worked in at xxxxx?**

   Plenty – industrial relations at the factory, management development, sales – as a rep!!!, marketing in Foods and

PC and HC, brand development and brand building locally, category director on both HPC categories, global brand directorship with 29 key countries as my playground when based in London. It's been great!

4. **How do you make a difference to South Africa?**

    I try to make a difference in many ways – firstly by leading a business that makes a difference to many peoples' lives – both through our brands and our people and the number of people who benefit from our business. Secondly, I'm involved in a number of joint business working groups with government and labour, where we're trying to address some of the big obstacles and opportunities facing the continued success of our business. And finally on a personal basis, because I believe so strongly in the democracy we have created and the future potential of our South Africa, I try to find each and every opportunity in personal interaction to positively influence our progress... Did you know that just positively engaging with a person who is job hunting or who is HIV positive can have an incredible ripple effect!

5. **What was the last thing you did that made you go 'YEEEEEESSSSS'?**

    Five things today:

    1. *I read that we had beaten our main competitor in a selected store with some strong promotional activity.*

    2. *I ran along the beach and made it up that dreadful hill without stopping until I got to the top.*

    3. *I made my grumpy teenage son laugh, instead of beating his brother.*

    4. *I noticed that my tree orchid is rooting and has a beautiful purplish-pink bloom.*

5. I helped my youngest reach level 3 of Orc in the Nations computer game.

I want a few more before I go to bed tonight!!

6. **What CDs are you playing in your car?**

Aria Classics (I love Opera), the Black Eyed Peas... for my boys (but I quite fancy them if I can block out the foul language sometimes), Green Day (same reason), Filippo (an Italian Opera singer), Il Divo (another Italian Operatic collection) and Rihanna (which I put in for my husband and I never play it cos I don't like it).

7. **What's your favourite TV programme?**

NCIS, the News, Supersport, Discovery, the Fishing Channel and good movies.

8. **What habit do you have that drives your secretary/ spouse/partner crazy?**

Determination – sometimes like a dog with a bone – and dreaming, when I go to my own planet...

9. **What do you enjoy doing when you have spare time?**

Having fun with my family, friends and dogs – tennis, golf, the beach, running and gym, fly-fishing, reading and reading and reading, cooking exotic dishes, travelling and gardening.

10. **What are two things you'd never leave home without?**

My clothes and my sense of humour

11. **Do you have a motto you live by?**

Live a life of significance and BE happy!

On- and off-the-record comments

This is a potential minefield when it comes to interviewing. The danger lies in clarifying exactly what is and isn't 'off the record'.

There's sometimes a problem distinguishing between the two. When does the 'off the record' end and 'on the record' start again?

Very often an 'OTR' comment can be followed up with another source and your interviewee.

Also check before turning on your tape recorder if the interviewee is happy about your using it.

Telephone interviewing

If you just need an interview with someone as 'part' of a larger story and seeing them doesn't add any value to your story then a telephone interview is the answer.

Some useful hints here are:

- Even if you're under extreme pressure don't let this show
- Be more than prepared – have pen and notebook ready, as well as questions
- Talk easily; don't tighten up your throat
- Introduce yourself right away and clearly:

    "Hi, this is James Kadzere here from xxxxxx... how are you? I'm doing an article on... and I wonder if you'd have a few minutes to speak to me...

- If you can manage some small talk this also helps to relax the interviewee

- Explain the story you're doing

- Brief the interviewee about what you expect

- Speak clearly and don't um and ah

- Be approachable and yet confident

- Repeat anything you're not sure of at the end

- Say yes, or grunt in agreement every now and again – the interviewee will then know there is someone listening and tell you more

Here again, a recording app on a phone or tablet will come in handy when used with the speaker on.

What not to ask

Almost nothing, although remember that this could be the end of a perfect interview. If the interviewee walks out because you've pushed too far, then you come away empty handed. This is where intuition comes in.

Although you will have drawn up a list of questions be prepared for your interview to take several other twists and turns.

Beware of the side-tracker. This is the person who is determined to take the interview firmly where they want it to go. That's anywhere, except where you want it to go. Make sure you steer it back in that direction.

Have certain points/questions that you **must** get answered and make sure you don't come away empty handed.

Last but not least

Make sure you get accurate contact numbers, especially cell numbers where you don't have to go through a secretary. This will be useful if you need to check anything with the interviewee at a later date.

POPULAR NEWSLETTER ARTICLES

How-to articles

These are often on issues such as filing your tax returns or following a particular new company policy or even teaching you some new skill.

One of the best ways to illustrate these articles is literally by 'illustrating' them. Use photos, graphics or drawings to show, for instance, awareness of breast cancer:

How to check for breast cancer

One in eight women will be diagnosed with breast cancer in her lifetime – but the good news is that if it's diagnosed early the outcome can be a positive one.

What is breast cancer?

Breast cancer is caused by cancerous cells in the breasts that often spread to the lymph nodes* in the armpits and sometimes other parts of the body.

What causes it?

- Genetics – family history

- Age – common over fifty

- Oestrogen – obesity, early menstruation, late menopause, hormone replacement therapy and the pill, meaning higher levels of the hormone oestrogen increasing their chances

Checking for cancer

Look for:

- Lumps, bumps or masses in the breast or armpit
- Discharge from the nipple
- Changes in the skin of the breast or nipple (dimpling, wrinkling, dryness, redness)
- Pain or changed sensation in the breast
- Examine each breast and armpit regularly
- Any changes should be checked by your doctor.

Mammograms

Mammograms are a specialised x-ray used to screen for breast cancer. All women over 40 should have regular mammograms.

Treatment

Depending on severity, treatment may include:

- Surgery – removal of the lump or breast to remove the cancer
- Chemotherapy – chemicals that fight cancer are used to shrink or destroy the cancer
- Radiation – special forms of x-ray beams are used to shrink the size of the tumour
- Hormonal treatments – medications to suppress oestrogen are used to prevent cancer growth

This story would really have benefited by illustrations on checking for lumps.

See this difference in the following story on exercising in the office.

Lifestyle

How to exercise in the office

You know you need to do more exercise but with your work schedule you just don't have time for gym. Well, now there's an answer with 'Office Aerobics' – check this out…

EASY OFFICE EXERCISES & WARMING UP INFOGRAPHIC

Company sporting events

All you need here are some good photos – generally of the victorious team with captions giving the names of the team. People LOVE to see their faces in their company newsletters.

Company courses and events

Again all you need are good photos with captions explaining what the photos are about. For instance:

The marketing team show off their well-earned certificates from their IMM Course on digital marketing. From left to right...

Message from the chairman or CEO

This is always a tricky one to navigate if you're the person putting the newsletter together. Your CEO might have a lot to say – much of which the staff aren't really interested in or the CEO may just not be a great writer. What you have to get across to him or her is that this isn't the vehicle through which to lecture your staff. This is the place to motivate and encourage – in as brief a way as possible.

The ideal situation here is for you to be given the threads of the column and you fill in the gaps before getting it cleared with the chairman.

EXAMPLE

A motivating CEO message

The last few months have seen us celebrating Women's Day – a time when here at xxxx we acknowledged, in the words captured in Maya Angelou's poem, 'phenomenal women' and our own phenomenal women. Our mothers, grandmothers, colleagues and friends – we celebrated both the importance and honour of being a woman, which shouldn't be honoured for just a day but 365 days a year.

We were also honoured to have a visit from Asia AMET, Central and Eastern Europe (AACEE) President, xxxxx, who motivated us with his words reminding us that although our economy is taking a hammering we must celebrate the small wins and the big ones will surely follow. See more about his visit on page ...

Even though times have been tough economically, which we're reminded of daily in our media, we know that our organisation can stand up to these knocks and with our concentration this year firmly fixed on delivering all round Customer Service Excellence each and every day, we are seeing growth. But we can't sit back and must strive even further in our efforts to offer our customers the ultimate service experience and make our company the supplier of choice.

EXAMPLE

A demotivating letter from the CEO

We've just turned five!

In real terms, at five years of age one is still a child and in my view so is the company. This is however not the perception from our strategic stakeholders. All of them expect maturity and a sense of clear direction from us. This means that we can no longer hide behind the fact that we're still young. The demands on us are enormous – for instance, International HQ expects full compliance to all systems and procedures, full respect for all the rules and regulations they set up and expect us to fully monitor our business operations as well as offering support and the necessary guidance to our customers, dealer network and suppliers. My question is: are we organised enough to stand up to these expectations? The answer is NO and believe me this is certainly not meant to sound negative. I have noted that there are good intentions, passion and that everyone is striving to do their best, but in certain instances, procedures are not being properly followed. This doesn't imply that things are not working; it's simply an acknowledgement that in order to grow further in a market that is fiercely competitive, we have to fully respect our own rules, and we also need to approach these rules with commitment.

It's time to move on to another phase now – another mode of operating – and everyone needs to make that switch to ensure even more success. Our sales are moving steadily along and our blue boxes are expanding. We therefore need to:

- Focus on after sales

- Pay more attention to quality issues

- Offer the right support to our dealer network

- Be more reliable with our forecast

We need to apply a sense of personal pride to everything we do, be it talking to a client on the phone, writing a letter to a supplier or running an event. We also need to follow standard procedures to ensure consistency. We need to intensify our efforts to attain all of the above. I need to emphasise that the right behaviour has a direct bearing on growth.

Happy anniversary…

COLUMN WRITING

You could have regular columns each issue in fields you think might interest your staff such as personal finance, health, cooking or cars. You might even find some staff members who are good at writing back-page humour columns. These are often the first pages people turn to.

Advice column

This can either be a fun thing or serious. To be a serious advice column you would need a resident psychologist or counsellor and then you would need staff members to actually write in – a very difficult task.

Health column

An essential for any company newsletter. Each issue should tackle a different illness, such as heart disease, diabetes, depression, etc. Here you can take a certain amount from the internet but even better if you have a company wellness programme that you can draw from.

 EXAMPLE

Stress – is it getting you down?

When you wake up on a Monday morning do you get that feeling in the pit of your stomach at the thought of another stress-filled week? Maybe you should start looking at ways to 'balance' your life.

When you spend more time at work than at home, you miss out on a rewarding personal life. On the other hand, if you're trying to cope with marital, financial or legal problems, you may find it hard to concentrate on your job. To find a balance between these two important areas of life, you first have to examine your priorities and set boundaries. Sometimes it's necessary to work really long hours to keep on top of things at work and with technology today you're always accessible. Be firm in what you can and can't do.

Here are a few tips to help:

Prioritise: *If you can't do everything (and few people can), do the most important things. This means deciding what the most important things are in your life: Your family life, social life, working life. To do this, you'll have to accept that some things are less important than others (and some people never manage this). Do these priorities match the time you spend on them? If not, you have found a really good place to start.*

Plan: *You need a diary/calendar, keep it updated and refer to it all the time.*

Exercise: *Don't forget to enjoy yourself – you deserve it. According to Dr John Lang, an expert on creating work-life balance and author of the book* Re: Life, *taking the time to exercise or have a hobby helps manage stress. After all, it's very difficult to think about what's worrying you when you're chasing a soccer ball.*

Exercise also increases the level of 'feel good' hormones and chemicals in your brain.

Studies show that people who exercise display lower levels of anger and hostility and higher levels of calmness than couch potatoes. Exercise also has an antidepressant effect similar to those provided by commonly prescribed drugs like Prozac.

Don't see crises as unsolvable problems: *You can't stop highly stressful events happening, but you can change how you interpret, respond to and accept them. Look beyond the present to how the future could be a little better, knowing nothing ever stays the same.*

Accept change as part of life: *Accepting things you can't change can help you focus on those you can change.*

Develop some realistic goals: *Take actions regularly – even if it seems like you're taking small steps – that enable you to move toward your goals. Instead of focusing on tasks that seem unachievable, ask yourself: "What is one thing I know I can accomplish today that helps me move in the direction I want to go?"*

Develop a positive view of yourself: *Developing confidence in your ability to solve problems and trusting your instincts helps build resilience.*

Learn to breathe: *When you're stuck in traffic, checking your watch as you struggle to get to work, your breathing may get shallow, your pulse rate high and your chest tight. In fact, you may feel this way in various situations… Sound familiar?*

If you're on a busy highway, pay attention to what's going on around you, but pay attention to your breathing, too. It's one of the few things you can control.

"Focusing on your breathing is one of the most effective ways of reducing stress," says cardiologist James Rippe, author of 10 books on health and fitness, including Healthy Heart for Dummies. *"It brings you into the here and now, distracting you from your worries."*

For more information call …

HUMOUR

This is often the first page people go to. Either you can invite staff members to write about funny things that have happened in their life or you find a permanent columnist in your office who just has the gift of writing humour.

The secret of humour writing is to take everyday situations and then quite simply take them over the top – but not so far as to be ridiculous.

A few ideas:

- Living with a sick spouse. How pathetic men are when they are sick – my husband made a great model for this

- A humorous look at what a woman's average day looks like compared with her husband's, who thinks he works hard

- Communication – how women communicate better than men. Example: When men talk to each other on phone and you say "So how was Bob?" (after your husband and Bob have spoken for about 15 minutes) and he replies "Fine." If we don't speak to our friends several times a week then there's so much to share. This also applies to the way they communicate with you or not...

- The appliance plot – when your appliances turn against you

- The housesitter – this could be a personal account of how to get a home wrecked in four weeks

- Political correctness – how not calling someone 'fat' but rather 'horizontally challenged' – can become totally ridiculous

- Supermarket trolleys – everyone looks in each other's at the checkout and it's amazing what their contents you can tell about someone

- Internet dating – that goes wrong

- The different ways men and women navigate a journey

Example from the best back-page writer in the world – Dave Barry:

The most powerful force in the universe is not any kind of nuclear energy. It is not magnetism, gravity or the IRS. The most powerful force in the universe is hormones. If you don't believe me, conduct the following simple scientific experiment:

1.   Take a normal woman.

2.   Get her pregnant.

3.   See if she can walk past a display of baby shoes without stopping.

I've been conducting this experiment for several months now with my wife, Michelle. She's pregnant, and I have reason to believe that I'm the father. I'm excited about this, because I'm at an age – 52 – when many of my friends are thinking about retiring to dull, meaningless lives of travel, leisure, recreation and culture. Not me! I'm about to start all over again with a brand-new little Miracle of Life to love, nurture and – above all – become intimately familiar with the poops of.

But so far the big change in my life has been Michelle's behaviour. She has never been a particularly maternal person; she's a professional sportswriter who has always been one of the guys. She understands the triangle offense and can watch football longer than I can. I've seen her fight her way through frenzied locker-room media mobs to get quotes from giant, sweaty football players. I've seen her stand on the field of 3Com Park in San Francisco right before a baseball playoff game, arguing in Spanish and not backing down one millimetre from a professional baseball player who was (1) VERY angry about something she had written and (2) holding a baseball bat.

Like many career women, Michelle insisted that becoming a mother would not change her. She was going to be the same professional person, darn it! She was NOT going to turn into one of those women who babble obsessively about the baby and baby clothes and all the other baby fixin's. Above all, she was NEVER going to drive a minivan. Right.

I would estimate that, at the present time, my wife's blood supply is 92 percent baby-related hormones. Doctors often call hormones 'the Donald Trumps of the human body' because they are moody, and when they give commands, they expect instant obedience. So for now my wife is not my wife: She is the official spokesperson for crazed dictator hormones. When the hormones wake up, they do NOT want an affectionate "good morning" kiss. They want AN UNCOOKED POP-TART, and they want it RIGHT NOW. You do not question them, because they will throw up on you.

The hormones also want baby shoes. I don't know why. I have seen the baby, at the doctor's office, via a procedure called a "sonogram," and although, of course, I think it is a very beautiful and gifted child, it looks, more than anything, like a wad of gum. I frankly cannot imagine, given its current lifestyle in the womb, that footwear is a high priority.

But you try telling this to the hormones. They are CRAZY for baby shoes. My wife could be fleeing from an armed robber, but if she ran past a display of baby shoes, her hormones would demand that she stop, pick up a shoe and exclaim to whomever is nearby, even the robber, "Look how CUTE!" The smaller the shoe, the cuter the hormones think it is. If somebody came out with a baby shoe the size of a molecule, which could be viewed only through a very powerful microscope, my wife's hormones would make her buy 27 pairs.

The hormones also want baby outfits. Even though the baby is still deep inside my wife and would be very hard to dress without surgical instruments, it already has at least as many outfits as a Kardashian. If you come to our house for any reason, including to fix an appliance, the hormones will make my wife show you these outfits one at a time, and as each one is held up, you will be expected to agree that it is cute.

Lately, the hormones have become obsessed with the decor of the baby's room. They definitely wanted a Winnie the Pooh theme, but they spent weeks agonizing over whether to go with the Regular Pooh or the Classic Pooh theme. They finally decided on Classic Pooh, but, of course, now they must decide which of the estimated 14 million Classic Pooh baby-room accessories they will need. This is an important issue, and the hormones think about it all the time, even during football games. Any day now, Michelle is going to walk up to a defensive tackle in the Miami Dolphins locker room and ask him what he thinks about the Pooh ceiling border. This is not her fault. She is merely the vehicle: The hormones are driving.

Speaking of which, they want a minivan.

VOX POPS

Or *vox populi* – the voice of the people – can be a good closer for an internal newsletter. Why not choose a different topic or question each issue and then go around your company and ask their opinion. Then you use their photo with a voice bubble giving their answer. Ask some staff members what they think about a 'working from home' option...

GETTING YOUR STAFF TO GIVE YOU NEWS

"I've asked them for news but I never get it," is the refrain I get from nine out of ten companies when the comms team are tasked with getting news from the various departments. So what's the secret – how do you get news from your colleagues?

Look at it from their perspective – it's a drudge. They've already got more than enough work and now that stupid woman from comms wants to give them more! The answer? Make it easy for them. Maybe email them some questions where they just have to fill in short answers. Or ask if you could take them to lunch and go armed with a tape recorder. Failing this, try sitting outside their office with a lunchbox to show you're going nowhere until you get your article!

PHOTOS, CAPTIONS AND ILLUSTRATIONS

Try, where possible, to use only colour photos, graphics or illustrations – black and white looks old fashioned these days unless it's used on a very beautiful black and white shot. There's nothing to beat a great image and a large snappy headline to draw people to a page.

Captions

If you're showing a group of people then always make sure:

- You get the correct spelling of people's names and their job title
- You label them from left to right

If the picture is of a place or event then again make sure you get the spelling and description correct.

 # EXERCISE

Writing headlines/headings

Headings should grab the reader's attention and give them a **complete** idea of what the story is about. Don't use more than five words, and if you can get it in two or three, even better.

Try your hand at the following:

- A story about teaching people to get out of debt
- A story on the latest electric car
- A story on beating sexual harassment in the workplace

Angles

The crux of journalism. Looking at the 'same old, same old' in a fresh way.

Try and find two angles for each of the following:

Carbon footprints

Controlling rodents

Pension funds

Aids

Headings

Headings should grab the reader's attention and give them a **complete** idea of what the story is about. Don't use more than five words and if you can get it in two or three, even better.

Try your hand at the following:-

- A story about teaching people to get out of debt
- A story on the latest electric car

EXTERNAL NEWSLETTERS

Newsletter or snoozeletter?

As with internal newsletters the size of the newsletter will vary from company to company. Some will be a one-pager a month. Others a 24-pager every four months. Much of what appears above applies to an external newsletter. Except for one thing – the audience is different and they need to know those aspects of what you're doing that will affect their lives. They are not too interested in the fact that Susie from accounts has had twins or that Moosa from Human Resources was promoted.

What kind of news do stakeholders want?

Firstly, you have to know just who you're writing for. If you're a medical aid company then you're looking at your clients, who hopefully want to stay healthy, so need tips in that direction and to know what you're doing to improve their service.

If you're a chain store then your customers will want to know about any upcoming special offers or even see a celebrity column or two.

Letter from the CEO, president or executives

What they don't want to see is the CEO droning on for a few pages on how great the company's achievements are. Show us rather than tell us, you would think. They need to hear from the boss but it shouldn't be more than a one-pager (if that) and naturally needs to be upbeat.

Company news

This is where anything NEWSWORTHY – really newsworthy – about your business or industry needs to reach your customers. That you've just been awarded a great new export contract or that you're branching out into new areas or opening new offices. This is worth writing about.

Success stories of customers

If you're a gym, for instance, and some of your members have competed and been placed in marathons or if you have a scientific product and have been able to change lives – people need to know. Today people love receiving news via real stories and photos.

Testimonials

It never hurts to read about success stories around your products or service – showing just what a great company you are and strengthening the image of your brand.

Profiles

Again, as in internal newsletters it doesn't hurt to highlight your staff to show the human side to your business. This can be anything from how someone who started out as a tea lady is now finishing her undergraduate studies and working as a PA or a story about one of your executives who does amazing NGO work in their spare time.

CSI

Again, as in your internal newsletter, it really helps for your customers to know that you don't just care about making profits, but that you're giving back to the community. This is also a great visual opportunity to show photos of any CSI events you've been involved in.

Human interest stories

If you ask any consumer magazine editor what their readers turn to first they'll tell you that apart from what Prince William and Kate or Beyoncé are doing, it's always the human interest stories. These can centre around someone in the organisation; again your CSI work or perhaps someone your company has helped, either in business or their personal life. This, together with good pictures, creates a lot of interest and possible Facebook posts and Twitter links. That is, of course, if you also use an online newsletter.

Industry news

This is where you get the chance to tell your customers about any new developments in your industry. Maybe some great research breakthroughs or perhaps a radical change in legislation. It could be an international development that would at some point have an impact on how you do business.

Company news

It goes without saying that this is the perfect vehicle for anything your business has done that's newsworthy. It could be that representatives of your company attended an international trade show or conference, bringing back the latest innovations in your industry, that you're relocating to new premises or that you headhunted a superstar from a rival company who's going to bring their talent and skills to your organisation.

Educational articles

These could relate to articles/blogs you have on your website offering advice/information on how to get the best out of your business/ products. As in internal newsletters, people love 'how-to' columns.

Blogs

Again, if you have a blog section on your website, this is the ideal place to reprint either the most popular blog posts since the last newsletter (with links back to your blog if online).

CASE STUDY: Barclays Africa Newsletter

This goes out to Premier Banking customers in 11 countries and what we've done is to tailor a certain amount of the content to the particular country it goes to as well of course as the images used. For instance, with Egypt we use different images to those used in Mauritius as some of the bank offerings only apply to certain regions which is where content also has to be tailored.

Alison Job, Online content marketing editor, ITweb.

EXERCISE

- What are the issues to take into consideration when putting together an internal/external newsletter?

- Name the steps you would take in order to ascertain whether electronic or hard copy would be more appropriate.

| |
| |
| |
| |
| |

CHAPTER 6

MARKETING DOCUMENTS

There are many people out there who call themselves marketers. Some even have impressive titles and letters after their name. But does that make them competent? Does it guarantee they are the go-to guys for increased business? Definitely not. So how can you firstly get your foot in the marketing door and then make sure you live up to your promises?

Alternatively you may have to draw up a marketing proposal in-house for a particular project or to increase sales or reach new markets for your company.

DRAWING UP A MARKETING PROPOSAL

Generating interest

Whether you're writing this within an organisation or as an agency trying to get new business, the marketing proposal is the key to making the right impression and showing you know how to take a business forward through marketing.

It's also the yardstick by which your performance will be measured, so it's not a time to make false claims or offer unrealistic outcomes. A strong marketing proposal should not only open doors for you but lay the groundwork for your ongoing relationship with your client.

If you're trying to break into a company, make no mistake, you're up against stiff opposition. Some marketing agencies are in a completely different league to you and others smaller than you. Very often, companies are going for the smaller, boutique agencies rather than the large multi-nationals. It's not always about the size of your company but the real research, energy and time you spend preparing for your pitch.

After all, if you can't persuade the client that you'll make a difference to their business, how can you think you can win over their customers?

Another good idea is to specialise. For instance, if you have knowledge of the pharmaceutical industry, then make your name within its ranks. The same for entertainment, art of wherever your expertise lies. The client will immediately pick up that your knowledge of their industry goes deep.

Many people feel it's all about undercutting the competition, but discerning clients are willing to pay and pay well for one thing – professionalism and real deliverables.

The proposal

Your proposal has to grab the client's interest from the first line to the last and a good tip here is to organise a meeting to deliver the proposal in person. There's nothing better than sitting around a table with clients, giving them an overview of what you're offering, before you hand them any written proposal. If you give them the proposal before you start talking they'll do what all prospective clients do – turn to the financials first.

You have a very short window of opportunity to sell yourself and your ideas here. A potential business relationship can easily die before it even takes off... This means: be confident, don't waffle and get to the point. All any client really wants to know is: what's in it for me and how can I get more out of my business?

Cover page

Remember, you get one chance to make the client even look at your proposal, let alone open it and distinguish it from the pile of proposals they've received. This means that your cover needs to have a strong visual appeal, preferably featuring your potential client's brand. Right from here on you need to show that this is all about the client and his problems – not your company.

Executive Summary – signposting the way

Right up front in your proposal, the client needs to quickly see that you've done your homework. That you understand their needs and problems and have a clear plan to resolve these. Then simply tell them how much you look forward to working with them to attain these goals and in as few words as possible tell them why your company is the right one for this project.

It's all about the client

As much as the client has to know something about you and your expertise, don't forget a marketing proposal is about the client's particular needs and how you can meet these. They're not really interested in:

> *"We started out in 2001... We have 16 years' experience in .... We... We... blah blah blah."*

They need to be convinced you fully understand their situation – otherwise, how can you help them solve their problems and issues? And, even more importantly, what are they going to get for their money in terms of results for their company?

How to sell it

The eternal question in marketing proposals is:

- What should I put in?

- What should I leave out?

- How do I make it flow and meet the client's expectations?

Research

Even though you may not get the contract make sure you do your research on the company concerned. Get them to give you as much information as possible on what they've done in the past and where they want to go in the future. Visit their premises, if possible, and see for yourself how their business runs. The time spent on this could make the difference between you getting the job or not.

Starting at the very beginning, when you're asked or have the opportunity to present a marketing proposal, what do you need to know?

- What are the company's goals, both financially and in terms of growth?
- Who are their target customers – who do they want to reach in terms of demographics (age, gender, interests, needs etc.)?
- What resources do they have to meet their current goals?
- What challenges have prevented them from reaching these goals?
- Are there other priorities that take precedence over reaching these goals?
- Can these be revised?
- What would be the cost if nothing changes?
- Are they using digital marketing at all?
- Are they using digital marketing in the most optimal way?
- Where does their pricing stand in terms of their competitors?
- And most importantly: How do they want their proposal presented?

On this last question you might find several answers such as:

- A one-pager outline will be fine initially
- Include all the services you're offering for the price
- Give me three case studies of other marketing campaigns you've been involved in with references
- We will send you standard supplier templates to be filled in

USP – unique selling proposition

The company's unique selling proposition or what makes them stand apart is critical when researching what differentiates them from their competition. Whether it's that their staff go more than the extra mile, that their safety record is immaculate or, hopefully, their product or service stands apart in their field, you have to know this before drawing up your proposal.

Once you've done your own research you could go into other areas such as whether they have to cut back on staff or whether the business is relying on this marketing plan to save it.

Opening – problem statement

As stated earlier in this chapter winning this account will largely depend on whether you grab the client's attention from the start. In the case of a marketing proposal this is the problem statement. This is where you show you've done your homework and understand the company's problems and needs.

And this means opening with a solution in a nutshell that you can expand on as you go along. Just putting in something straight out of Marketing 101 won't do and would perhaps look like this:

Over the last three years xxxx Company have seen a sharp decrease in over-the-counter sales and are seeking new ways to increase their turnover. We recommend a digital marketing strategy embracing social media and utilising strong SEO, together with a minimum six-month management, research and analytics programme.

 This is simply telling the client what they already know – that they need to up their digital game – but doesn't get to the heart of the problem i.e. why they need more online traffic.

Solving their problems

You need to show them you understand their problems and then lay out in clear language just how you plan to solve them:

Over the last few years more and more of xxxx Company's clients have become online shoppers, seeing less feet through their stores, taking their business to competitors' websites.

Xxxx Company needs to focus on eCommerce to regain market share with a strong digital campaign boosting SEO (search engine optimisation) and PPC (pay per click) initiatives, monitored with monthly research and analytics reports to monitor sales.

We recommend a marketing strategy using paid Facebook ads and extensive use of Twitter to drive users to your company's website. The ROI for similar ads in your company's niche is 7:1 making them extremely cost effective. We also recommend optimising your website for high-volume keywords to drive free traffic for months and years to come.

This immediately shows that you've got to the heart of their problems and can come up with a resolution. Most companies won't even realise where their problem areas lie, particularly when it comes to using digital marketing. If you want to produce a winning proposal you need the client to know your company is the one that really understands their needs.

When it comes to talking digital don't assume your client understands this language and make sure you explain any acronyms such as SEO and PPC (as above).

Fee schedule

Often the first page a prospective client will turn to and one that must be completely clear at first glance.

Your pricing must make sense and how you show this on your proposal could make you stand apart from your competition.

 **EXAMPLE**

Service Item	Cost
Discovery – Assessing your current marketing strategies, where your customers are in the market place and identifying new opportunities	R
Branding – Gaining a clear understanding of your business and long-term goals to drive that vision into a marketable brand	R
Marketing strategy for online and offline media – Customising a strategy to reach new prospects across traditional as well as digital platforms	R
Getting into the digital space – Setting out a way forward to reach your current and potential clients online using your website as well as social media	R
Total	R

Covering letter

You have put a lot of effort into crafting your proposal but it's not over yet. Many people make the mistake of attaching the proposal to a skimpy covering letter or email as a mere formality. This is a big mistake. Remember, your covering letter is as important, if not more important, than your proposal because if it doesn't impress, your proposal is likely never to be opened. It's the hook to land your client and has to create enough interest to make them want to read further. This doesn't mean multiple paragraphs – to the contrary, get to the point fast and leave them wanting more…

MARKETING AGREEMENT

Drawing up a marketing agreement

There are many different kinds of marketing agreements, depending on the parties involved, the size of the project and legal aspects. These agreements are essential to clarify the purpose and conditions of the arrangement for both parties, safeguarding both the provider and the company receiving the services.

The legal side

By simply going online you can download many different templates that will help you with these agreements and lay out the legalities. The main ones being to:

- Identify the parties involved in the agreement

- Give the title or company of each person represented in the contract

- State the full address of both parties

- State the date both parties accepted the agreement

Terms and Termination

This states the exact length of time involved in the agreement (six months, one year) and the breakdown of marketing duties as well as how each party can terminate the agreement. This is vital because it specifies the execution of the contract. For example, a company entering into a marketing agreement with a public relations agency may require content to be accepted only after approval by the company's marketing department. The agency may also require the company to give 30 days' notice before terminating the agreement.

Services, Fees and Compensation

Fees
(What one pays)

Value
(What one gets)

Here the agreement shows what marketing services have been requested and how these will be provided to meet these requests. It also lays out the scope of work, how one party will be paid for this requested work and how any additional costs may be involved if the contract goes over the services initially agreed. Terms of payment can also be laid out here.

Confidentiality and Intellectual Property

Today, particularly with identity theft being such a large threat, many marketing agreements have a clause protecting client data, passwords and any sensitive information. They may also cover who owns what after the agreement expires.

MARKETING STRATEGY

You've been awarded the contract and now the hard work really begins. First job is drawing up a workable marketing strategy. What are you looking at here?

Market Overview – competitors

Here you lay out just who their competition is and what part of the market share they hold.

Market Segments

Exactly which different markets the company wants to reach and which products will reach which market.

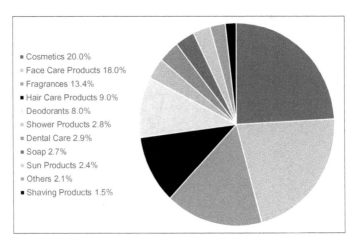

- Cosmetics 20.0%
- Face Care Products 18.0%
- Fragrances 13.4%
- Hair Care Products 9.0%
  Deodorants 8.0%
- Shower Products 2.8%
- Dental Care 2.9%
- Soap 2.7%
- Sun Products 2.4%
- Others 2.1%
- Shaving Products 1.5%

Target Markets

Here you will generally have several sectors such as primary, secondary and tertiary.

Segmentation for Netflix

Total # of customers – 200	Cluster 1	Cluster 2	Cluster 3	Cluster 4
Size	68	32	45	55
Age of Customer (Mean)	32	26	44	58
Gender (in %)				
Male	58%	47%	36%	64%
Female	42%	53%	67%	36%
# of children in Household (mean)	1.03	0.54	2.4	1.1
# of movies rented in last 3 months	10	12	3	8
Genre of movies rented in last 3 months (mean %)				
Action	30%	26%	18%	32%
Comedy	22%	31%	27%	20%
Child	20%	2%	32%	1%
Romance	4%	27%	3%	2%
Drama	15%	12%	15%	17%
War	9%	2%	5%	28%

Overview of key company requirements

- Market visibility
- Brand awareness
- National footprint

Overview of key challenges

- Current low profile in the market

- Lack of brand awareness

- Pricing

- Distribution issues

- Knowledge of target markets

- Internal cohesion

Proposed Messaging

Having studied and understood the company's core business and where they want to drive it, you can now show them how you would use their 'messaging'. This would vary in size depending on the project. There's no exact template here.

- Short statement or bullet points summarising benefits

- Short statement on what you bring to a target buyer

- What makes the product stand apart

- Example: Completely green product with minimal carbon footprint

Branding

Here, although branding may stand apart in some proposals, it ultimately affects any marketing. So, where you feel a company's branding as it currently stands would affect marketing, you must make recommendations:

- Corporate identity

  - Logo

  - Business cards, letterheads, email signatures, PowerPoint templates, fleet branding

  - Company headquarters branding

- Website

  - Mobile responsive, online order forms, social media integration, sales lead generator, SEO

  - Online sales tools – downloads of detailed specifications, price sheets and case studies

- Product packaging

- Label designs

SALES TOOLS

Show how you would help the client put together a catalogue/brochure that would:

- Grab attention

- Put them firmly in their marketplace

- Sell their products off the page

- Make it user friendly

- Price lists

- Point-of-sale banners

- Incentives

- Branded clothing

COMMUNICATIONS

- Paid-for advertising

  - Print media

  - Billboards

  - Photography/pack shots

- Advertorial

  - Paid-for editorial placements in suitable media/b2b (business to business)/consumer

- Public relations

  - Building executives into company/industry spokespeople

  - Organising media breakfasts with executives to build media relations

  - Identifying suitable media to target

  - Draw up six-month media plan

- Social media
  - Identify just which social media channels to use
  - Train suitable staff to channel news through social media
  - Set up regular news bytes/newsletters
  - Draw up Social Media Content Calendar
  - Produce YouTube videos/animation

CONTENT SCHEDULE

Whether this centres around social media, sales, media, or particular events in a company's calendar there's one thing you can't overlook: a carefully planned content calendar or schedule.

Firstly, if you're dealing with more than one group or team you're creating a useful alignment tool and secondly, and perhaps more importantly, you're keeping writers on track for their work. If you're not sure where to start there are some excellent free templates available online.

FORMAT

Generally Excel or Google spreadsheets would be the first choice but if there are other methods that suit your organisation then go with what works for you.

It could simply be in calendar form, either weekly or monthly, with as many columns as you need:

Date	Title	Publish date	Content Type
Mon Jan 8, 2018	2018 Regional Planning	Mon 15 2018	Detailed report
Tues Jan 9, 2018			

Date	Title	Publish date	Content Type
Wed Jan 10 2018	Strategic Communications Outline	Thurs 25 2018	Excel
Thurs Jan 11 2018			
Fri Jan 12 2018	CEO's New Year Message	Tuesday 16 2018	Long-form Blog Post

You could extend the content type to more than one column with events also included. You might also want to separate schedules for each type of content you're creating. For instance, one for a blog, another for an internal or external newsletter and others for reports, white papers or case studies. You will know just what you need to be able to clearly track your work progress.

If, for instance, you are writing an internal newsletter and you need contributions from various writers it may look like:

Post date	Author	Title	Keywords	Category	Tags	Status

By tracking keyword and tags you can make sure you have exactly what you need for SEO (Search Engine Optimisation) and digital optimisation and conversion.

Today no marketing strategy is complete without a social media marketing content which would have lines for each type of social media you're involved in:

N39	▼	fx					
A	B	C	D	E	F	G	H

SOCIAL MEDIA MARKETING CONTENT CALENDAR [YEAR]							
WEEK 1							
CHANNEL	MONDAY	TUESDAY	WEDNESDAY	THURSDAY	FRIDAY	SATURDAY	SUNDAY
FACEBOOK							
TWITTER							
PINTEREST							
LINKEDIN							
INSTAGRAM							
YOUTUBE							
VINE							
SLIDESHARE							
SNAPCHAT							
FOURSQUARE							
BLOG POST							
EMAIL NEWSLETTER							

CASE STUDY: From Tamsin Rankin, Marketing and Communication Specialist, Rankin Marketing

As all good estate agents say, when investing in a new home – location, location, location! A similar sentiment is true when embarking on a new marketing campaign for a client – research, research, research!

The more informed the marketer, the better equipped he or she will be in effectively launching a new brand or marketing campaign. Most clients don't have the budget to perform large-scale research – simple Q&As with the client and their internal and external teams, coupled with desktop research will aid greatly.

Recently I worked on the launch of a new energy brand within central Africa. Having never been onsite within this country and working towards exceptionally tight deadlines, my team decided on a simple solution – Google Maps! We utilized the Street View functionality to 'walk' through the major towns in that country. This, coupled with a series of questions to the local branch of the business on the ground, enabled us to broadly establish which brands, colours, shapes, etc appealed to local consumers.

This formed a solid base from which we were able to draw our initial creative briefs. This saved both us and the client on valuable time – as we were able to reach a design much more effectively and quickly. Most of all, we were able to create a brand with a look and feel which was respectful and appealing to the local, conservative market – and one which clearly showcased the primary offering of the new energy brand. Simple, clean and effective.

Having worked on numerous re-branding and new branding projects over my 14 years in the industry – spanning retail, FMCG, and energy sectors – what this story highlights is the need for a calculated approach when commencing work on any project, no matter the scale.

 EXERCISE

Draw up a social media content calendar for the launch of a new property app, where people will be able to either rent or buy straight off their phone. Show how the use of different sites would be applicable for different marketing content.

SECTION 2: EXTERNAL COMMUNICATION

CHAPTER 7

DEALING WITH CUSTOMERS' ENQUIRIES AND COMPLAINTS

Isn't it strange how when you first want to do business with a company they generally can't do enough for you, but when it comes down to getting detailed information out of them you often find yourself waiting and waiting and...

Many companies in fact openly brag about their superior customer service – and those very same companies are generally the ones who fall short when it comes to delivering.

The same overall rule to writing anything applies here as with anything else in the digital mindset – short and sweet.

ENQUIRIES

FOLLOW-UP

PHONE   DIRECT MAIL   E-MAIL   MEETING   DOCUMENTS   NOTES

CONTACTS

As discussed in Chapter Four writing styles have changed dramatically with the use of technology and digitalisation. Today many companies deal with enquiries received online but that doesn't take away from the basics of replying efficiently and timeously.

An initial enquiry may be just that, a first communication to establish whether you can in fact help them in a particular area. Your reply may look like this:

Thank you for your enquiry regarding our machine hiring division. We're attaching a copy of our rates and services.

If you could send us more details on your exact needs we'll be able to give you a more detailed quote. We look forward to doing business with you.

Many thanks.

Kind regards,

That's quite a basic reply. If your company has a lot of competition in a particular field you may want to offer an even better service and your reply would then look like this:

We received your inquiry about hiring some machinery from us and we appreciate your interest.

We're attaching a copy of our rates and services for you to look over but would be happy to get one of our sales people to call and give you more detailed information.

They could also organise a visit to our showroom so you could see first-hand the quality of our machines.

We look forward to doing business with you and hope to hear from you soon.

Kind regards,

And then there's really going the extra mile:

Thank you for your order to hire two hydraulic breakers which will, as requested, be delivered within the next 24 hours.

Before we do this we wanted to confirm the exact entrance you wanted them delivered to, as we notice your premises has several entry points.

Should you have any other queries please don't hesitate to call me.

Thanks again for your order. We look forward to your final instructions.

Kind regards,

Response to an email inquiry for information:

Thanks for your enquiry about the writing courses listed on our website. Before we are able to recommend the right course for your employee we'd like to know more about your specific needs.

1. *What type of day-to-day writing do they do? Website content, business letters, blogs?*

2. *What level of English competency do they have?*

3. *Are they involved in public relations for your company?*

4. *Are they competent in using graphics?*

Once again, thank you for your interest in our courses and I'm sure we'll be able to find a course to suit your employee's exact needs.

Don't hesitate to call me should you want further information.

Kind regards,

Key points to remember

- Respond to customers' requests or queries quickly to prove they are a priority
- Write a sincere reply which will instantly set you apart from your competition
- Mention the client's request
- Tell them how you've handled this

- Give any information they have asked for and attach any information that will illustrate this

- Explain how they can order (if this is the case) and let them know you're there to answer any questions they may have

- End on a positive note

COMPLAINTS

Even the best of companies occasionally experience an irate customer and today, with social media 'spreading the word' so quickly, these complaints have to be handled before they become a Tweet. By the time you've dealt with the problem not only have you made the customer's problem go away but you have recruited an advocate for your brand.

South Africans as a whole are reluctant to complain – to the company concerned – but they have no problem telling the world at large how they feel. Research suggests up to 80% of customers are satisfied with the service they receive but you don't want to fall in the 20% who aren't! It's getting harder, not easier, to satisfy customers in today's world of instant gratification so you really have to go beyond the extra mile to earn loyalty.

A complaint successfully handled can literally turn an irate customer into the best ad your company could have. So what do you have to do?

If it's a telephone complaint, then listen carefully to what they have to say without interrupting and getting defensive. The same goes for an email/letter – read it in its entirety. Remember, it's never a personal attack. They have a problem and you're there to solve it.

Research shows that around 46% of consumers who have sent complaint letters don't receive satisfactory answers – or only some answers to their problem. This is because the person reading the complaint stops at the first point, answers that and ignores the rest.

A good idea to prevent this happening is to copy the customer's email and paste it into your reply back. That way you can answer each part without leaving anything out. Once you've done this you just delete the pasted paragraphs.

 EXAMPLE – Complaint letter

Dear ...

I'm writing to complain of the dreadful service I received from your company on 18 September 2017. I'd left work particularly early in order to meet your representative, Joe Soap.

Mr Soap was an hour late for our appointment and didn't even bother to apologise. To add to this he brought me completely the wrong samples to look at, even though I'd sent him the exact links on your website.

This meant that I had taken time off work without having achieved anything other than frustration.

I'm not sure now whether to proceed with your company if this is how you conduct business. I look forward to hearing from you.

Yours.......

Obviously this is one very unhappy 'prospective' customer and you have to think carefully before replying. Don't start with the generic 'We have received your email dated or your letter dated...' You're replying – so obviously you received their complaint. Rather write:

Thank you for taking the time to write to us about this really unfortunate incident. We appreciate it when customers let us know when things go wrong and give us the opportunity to fix this situation.

Most importantly, don't forget to actually apologise. This sounds obvious but is very often left off a reply. Companies are often afraid of admitting liability in a situation but apologising in an email isn't about placing blame.

An apology letter should also be seen as a marketing opportunity. It's a chance to show you really care for your customers and want to do whatever it takes to make a situation right.

Reply

Dear ...

Firstly we'd like to apologise for the incident that happened between you and ...... We have looked into the matter and would like to assure you that this will definitely never happen again. Unfortunately Mr xxxx is a new employee, and whilst this doesn't excuse what happened, he did make some basic errors.

We hope you will give us another opportunity, not only to meet with you but to make up for our lack of service. We would be happy to meet you at your home in or out of office hours – whatever suits you.

Once again, our sincere apologies.

Kind regards,

Accepting liability

This doesn't however automatically mean you have to accept responsibility for a situation until you've fully looked into the matter. What is important is to immediately get back to the customer to assure them you're listening and checking out the problem. Then you can either explain why or how the problem arose.

Compensation

If there is a refund involved, remember this. Whatever the cost it's going to be cheaper than the bad advertising you're going to get if the complainant goes onto social media. Your reward will be increased customer satisfaction, loyalty and the best word-of-mouth advertising you could ask for.

Daniel Munslow, CPRP, Independent Communication and Brand Consultant:

Stakeholder engagement is still the most useful way of connecting with external audiences. Being proactive and building trust, so leveraging authenticity during non-crisis periods, is very important. The public is increasingly more suspicious of content from organisations, as was illustrated in the 2017 Trust Barometer – www.Edelman.com/trust2017. This is something organisations need to take into account when building their engagement programmes.

Kevin Welman, Director, ByDesign Communications:

*There certainly isn't one 'best method'. Communicators have more tools and more channels available to them than ever before. Knowing **how** to use each channel and **when** is the key to any successful communications programme. But sticking* *to the basics is key; understand what the business is trying to achieve and why, what role can communications play against the business objectives, what do you need your targeted audiences to believe and how are you going to create the environment for them to believe. Simple. I find that most communicators and most businesses over complicate things.*

Kate Johns, Head, Africa Communications, Standard Bank:

I still feel that one-on-one engagement is the best way to pitch a story or angle to a journalist or social media influencer – knowing what they are interested in covering and knowing who their readership will reach. Increasingly, I am starting to see the use of "alternative" PR tools like podcasts, infographics, GIFs, well-captioned images, and tweet-friendly content being readily accepted by media – in other words, we are repackaging information that makes it media-friendly, instantly uploadable and ready for sharing. We're still sharing information (good solid, proof-read, triple-checked, relevant and engaging, interesting and factually correct!) in the two-way exchange integral to the art of media relations, we are just adopting a more modern approach

Solly Moeng, Managing Director and Senior Consultant, DonValley Brands, Marketing and Communications Agency:

All comms, internal and external, should be informed by a 360° understanding of the operational environment of the organisation (economic and socio-political). Communicators should also understand the stakeholder environment and the issues that matter to the organisation's stakeholders, e.g. environmental awareness, rights issues, labour issues, safety issues, etc. They should also understand the organisation's competitor environment, as it might also impact on or inform the content and tone of all communications leaving the organisation. Ultimately, communicators who don't know what's happening in the world around them and how all of that has/might have relevance for their organisation are, potentially, a liability for the organisation. Strategic communicators must be positioned to act not just as 'runners' or 'fire fighters' when there is trouble; they should be able to inform strategic decision-making processes upstream, not mid or downstream when it might be too late.

CASE STUDY: Ford fiasco – putting out fires

When it comes to first prize in getting communications wrong this has to be awarded to Ford over their mishandling of their Ford Kuga crisis. And yes, it was a crisis.

From the moment Reshall Jimmy died after his Ford Kuga caught fire near Wilderness in the Western Cape in December 2015, to the subsequent outcry of many other Kuga owners who also suffered engine fires due to faulty coolant systems, Ford couldn't have handled this worse.

Obviously acting on the advice of their lawyers and insurance company not to incriminate themselves over the Jimmy incident, they rather denied the possibility that the fault was Ford's in any possible way. But then, when around another 40 Ford Kuga models spontaneously combusted a year later, they were forced to issue media statements. By now those few hundred thousand Rands were starting to look like a great opportunity missed!

Even with this overwhelming evidence of a serious mechanical problem Ford remained tight-lipped and even arrogant over the issue, prodding the South African media and public to rise up in protest demanding action.

What's interesting to note here is whatever Ford spent in advertising across their various vehicles in a year was more than wiped out by this situation in around a few days. And we're not talking small money here.

By January 2017 they were forced to recall more than 4 500 Kuga Ecoboost 1.6 litre models. But by now it was too late – their reputation was in tatters.

So where did they go wrong – apart from the obvious?

Firstly by not dealing sympathetically with the distraught Jimmy family. There wasn't a single sympathetic note, email or, even better, phone call, offering sympathy to Jimmy's family and friends. Instead there was indignation that Ford could be remotely to blame for this incident.

What they should have done was immediately offered, without taking the blame, to cover any costs incurred in the crash, saying they would conduct an immediate investigation. This would at best have cost them a few hundred thousand Rands – not the thousands of millions it's now cost them in good will.

 **EXERCISE**

1. Name and discuss areas of vulnerability within companies' external communications which need constant attention from communications staff.

2. Which are the most vulnerable and what should always be the first consideration?

CHAPTER 8

REPORT WRITING

A recurring theme throughout this book is the way people read and take in content in the digital era. Companies today still write copious amounts of reports – often to the detriment of large forests. The question is perhaps: how many of these reports actually get read from start to finish, particularly annual general and quarterly reports? Taking into account the King IV Report on Corporate Governance for South Africa (2016), which emphasised integrated reporting and integrated thinking, this doesn't stop companies looking at new ways to present their reports.

This chapter takes a look at report writing as a whole, throwing in some new ways of tackling what are often onerous and dreaded jobs.

GENERAL REPORT WRITING

Planning and organising content

"My way is to start at the beginning." – Lord Byron

Before you write anything, draw up a plan of what you need to cover – either in note or even bullet form. If you don't know exactly what you want to say then how will the person receiving this report begin to understand what you're reporting on or possibly want from them in response?

Key writing points

Firstly, your writing needs to be clear and concise. Unlike a conversation, the reader can't ask questions if something isn't clear.

- Your writing will be judged in the same way you're judged on your manner, appearance and presentation when you speak. So, just as you'd think about your looks and manner, the same applies to the way your writing comes across.

- Having a clear approach to your writing is essential.

Ask yourself:

- **Who am I writing this for?** Always consider just WHO your audience is? Will the people reading this expect formal or informal language? How important will the use of photos or graphics be? Should this be just in print format or digital also?

- **Why am I writing it?** What do I want to accomplish? Do you want to provide information, argue a point of view, ask for input or give instructions? Do you have a single intention or several different intentions?

- **How am I going to present it?** Once you know what and why you're writing you should be able to form some ideas about the type of language you need to use and how you're going to present it. Is a lengthy explanation needed or will a quick summary do? Does the page need long, solid paragraphs, or will more white space look better? How about bullet points – would that be the best way to get information across? How about photos with captions or a digital format using video clips?

- **What response do I want?** Do you need an acknowledgement, a specific piece of information, feedback from your staff? Do you need to make this clear in what you write?

Once you've answered these questions you should have a firm idea of what you're setting out to do. You're now ready to make a start, but maybe not to write the finished product. The actual process of writing can be divided into four stages:

- Research

- Planning and thinking

- Drafting

- Revising/editing

Always consider how much time and patience your readers are prepared to give to your report:

- Will the use of more graphs make it easier for the reader than heavy text?

- What are the reading skills of my audience?

- Am I giving them enough/too much information?

- Are we overdoing the visuals and videos to the detriment of the material?

Some comments from people who regularly receive reports:

> "The report must meet the needs of the readers and answer the questions in their minds."

"The report must be at the right level for the readers. Some readers have an in-depth knowledge of the subject; others may be decision-makers."

"The report must have a clear, logical structure – with clear signposting to show where the ideas are leading."

"The report must not make assumptions about the readers' understanding. All writers need to apply the 'so what' test and need to explain why something is a good idea."

"The report must give a good first impression. Presentation is very important."

"All reports must be written in good English – using short sentences and with correct grammar and spelling."

Logical structure

You'll need to structure the content in a logical and clear way if you're going to help the readers take in your message.

Organise your ideas. Make sure you have a sequence of headings and sub-headings which act as signposts to help readers find the information they need.

Also, if you structure a piece of writing well, you'll find it easier to choose words to express your ideas. Where you need to emphasise issues such as 'pushing sales' in a particular area make sure this is given prominence in your report – make it stand out.

A report should be divided into sections and sub-sections, each of which should have a clear heading. If you structure a report well, it will not only help your readers find the information they need but also help you when you start writing.

Guiding your reader

| Make your report reader-friendly | Decide which direction to take the report – print/digital | Think of your reader – how would they benefit most? |

- Make sure you've covered every area of your business from staff to new directions

- Watch out for anything you don't know where to put – don't dump into 'general'…

- Use strong headings that clearly highlight what that section is saying

- Avoid repetition – check there's no overlap where you've used the same information in more than one section

- Don't overfill any one section – watch out for overdoing the headings. Try and stick to six points maximum per section.

Research

The key question – where do I start? Well, you can't start before you have ALL the information you need from every department involved. This can be frustrating as there are always people who let you down. Hound them. Literally be sitting outside their office as they arrive for work and tell them you're not leaving without the information you need…

Watch out for internet research. Just because you found it on Google doesn't mean it's factually correct. Check and double check your sources.

This is even more important when it comes to statistics. Always make sure you double check figures. You could look really bad if you quote incorrect figures for sales or any statistics.

If you feel you haven't been able to find all the information you need then find someone who can help you here. Don't start writing when your research is incomplete. And remember that all research stated needs to be referenced.

Drafting

It's always a good idea to start by either using bullet points or notes to help plan a layout for your report. Once you've done this for your introduction, body and conclusion you'll start seeing where everything should go. And again, it will stop that repetition.

Deciding on style

Formal or informal? Active or passive? Is there a standard you have to follow? Again, decisions to make before you start rather than have to change when you've finished. This will, of course, largely depend on whether the company concerned is the latest digital start-up gaming app, a fashion brand or a bank... No one size fits all.

Capture the reader's interest

As we've said in earlier chapters, keeping readers' interest today is difficult. You have the skimmers, readers and others. Again, the subject matter will also dictate here. If it's a bank and you're talking about how much they help their customers, then a great success story of how they helped a young couple buy their first home would work well. Or perhaps a short clip of your corporate social investment work, showing staff helping out at a crèche in an informal settlement. It's all about capturing and keeping people reading.

A danger point for losing readers is where you have to show statistics. The minute people are faced with numbers, especially within a paragraph, they're likely to turn the page. The only way you can get them to take notice of numbers is by using charts and graphs and putting any other info into words.

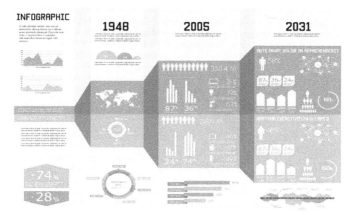

Tell your story visually

A picture paints a thousand words – especially in the digital world. With the onslaught of social media today people are becoming used to looking at a picture then reading what it's about. And with a report you're telling some type of story – whether it's around how well the company has done in a particular area or about the new direction the company's taking.

Ribbon cutting for the new Business Centre which will employ over 5 000 people opening in 2018

Taking the company to new global heights

Write captions that tell your story

Now that you've got them looking at the photos, tell a story with your captions. Don't just state what or who's in the photo. Connect the photo to an accomplishment. If people read nothing but the captions in your report, they should still get a sense of the good work you did.

Local branches making a real-life difference for the holidays.

Overcrowding

Don't try and fit too much information on a page. To be readable you need plenty of white space around the pictures and words. Go for a clean, open look.

ANNUAL GENERAL REPORTS

Most companies, especially major corporates, if asked to detail everything they have done over a year would come up with a book you'd need a forklift to carry. The beauty of living in the digital world is that we can so easily condense reports and documents to just highlight the real benefits and stories.

Perhaps the biggest problem here is keeping everyone happy – as they all want to see their name and work recognised in the report. To silence anyone who questions this, simply quote from the King III and King IV codes where they state:

> An integrated report is a concise communication about how an organisation's strategy, governance, performance and prospects, in the context of its external environment, lead to the creation of value over the short, medium and long term.

An honest report, of course, shouldn't just talk about the positives but also the negatives of the past year. It can then go on to say what is being done to overcome these situations, going away from the negatives to what people can look forward to in the coming year. Trying to brush anything bad under the carpet can often backfire badly.

On the other side of this, whatever is promised going forward in an annual general report is there for the public to see and note.

EXAMPLE – Complaint letter

The SABC's Annual General Report 2013/2014

Chairman at the time, Ben Ngubane stated that the 2011/2012 year had been "both a challenging as well as a rewarding year for all of us at the SABC". He went on to comment that things had progressed well with the second phase of the turnaround strategy regaining stability and how they were being prudent in spending and cost reduction, implementing strict financial and internal controls.

Ngubane went on to say "Crucially, the foundation has been laid for the corporation to continue to move towards meeting the government guarantee conditions and targets." As history has now told us, this never happened and year on year the SABC has sunk further into a financial and corporate governance quagmire.

Going the digital route

Up to now only a small group of forward-thinking companies and non-profit organisations have gone this route. Again, people want their information in bite-size chunks – not reams of text – and digital provides this. The big advantage here is that people can then access a digital version of your report from your website and perhaps, more importantly, suddenly your Annual General Report becomes a valuable marketing tool.

What are benefits of going the digital route?

- Speed and ease of reading, especially when giving complex information

- Making stories attractive for stakeholders and investors

- Being able to use this on company websites/mobisites (must be mobile friendly)

- Close connection through interaction with readers

- Can be flagged on social media

- Linked to pitches and presentations

- Using analytics allows you to measure how long people stay on a page

- Ability to portray stories in new and different formats such as:

  - Video – particularly effective in showing your CSI work

  - Animation

  - Social sharing functionalities

  - Podcasts

What are the dangers?

- Overwhelming readers with graphics and multimedia

- Too many bells and whistles – you're not making a movie trailer...

- Appearing frivolous with serious issues

- Possible technical issues in terms of downloading etc.

- Overlong videos that will take too long and use too much data to download

- Could end up costing more than the print version

This doesn't mean to say that digital will be better for every organisation. Again, it depends totally on your audience and goals. It doesn't however stop you from producing both a print and digital version of your report.

CASE STUDY 1

**Mandy Smith, Berenice van Dyk and Lorraine du Plessis –
Studio 5 Graphic Design**

*Bridging the gap between print and online when it comes to
integrated reports is an opportunity that companies are slowly
starting to recognise, explains the dynamic team at Studio 5
Graphic Design. Their client list comprises many top JSE Top 40
companies in South Africa so their experience in meeting their
clients' needs is vast.*

*"The traditional approach is to complete the printed version first,
and then produce the online report as a kind of second cousin,"
explains Berenice van Dyk, Client Services Director at Studio
5. "Because digital and printed reports should complement and
supplement each other, we encourage our clients to think about
them holistically up front, plan them together and then develop both
versions in alignment with each other. Those who have embraced
this approach are pleased with the results."*

KEEPING IT SIMPLE AND EASILY DIGESTIBLE

*Integrated reporting requires that reports be succinct and short,
so the online environment is becoming crucial as a repository for
additional or statutory information that is not included in the print
version. Consequently, clients are rapidly recognising the value of a
'hybrid' approach for the online report.*

*Online/digital offers additional opportunities to the printed document
and makes for a more immediate, interactive experience. This
includes providing salient information in clear, easy to digest
scrollable pages combined with animation, graphic elements or
videos. Furthermore, responsive web pages are device-agnostic,
allowing for easily accessible information on phones and tablets.*

This approach can be combined with downloadable PDF section/ pages which provide more complete information.

Hybrids can be more cost- and time-effective than providing an entire online website in html, which was the trend some years ago. However, some clients still prefer this approach.

"The Discovery Annual Report is a good example of the value of a hybrid approach," explains Mandy Smith, Director at Studio 5. "The online version is not simply a replica of the printed report, but has been designed in such a way that the most important information and key features are presented in individual pages with bite-sized sections of content which click through to the relevant PDF sections.

"In contrast, the online Discovery Sustainability Report was written specifically for web and the only links are to the print version PDF and to additional information such as GRI tables etc."

(We will do screen grabs of these reports to illustrate) in tandem, diff version for web) – This is from Studio 5!

"What works particularly well," says Smith, "is when there's a pop-up menu which enables readers to select key sections and print out only what is required – not the entire PDF."

The reporting of financial statements is also changing. Lorraine du Plessis, Managing Director of Studio 5 remarks that "One of our clients recently opted for a one-page online summary which incorporated links to PDFs for readers who wanted more detail, and this proved extremely successful. It's important to assess client needs and provide them with online solutions that meet requirements."

THE ULTIMATE REPORT

According to van Dyk, "The ultimate online report should undoubtedly include some interactivity, especially video which provides additional insight and immediate information. Not all clients are ready for this yet, as it necessitates a change of mindset and at the same time, print still has tremendous value. Some clients still want to hold and read the hard copy of a report. Online is a great tool for reference, visual experience, quick access and instant information."

"At the end of the day our aim is to provide a fit for purpose product; well thought out design and relevant content that go hand in hand whether online or in print," explains van Dyk.

CASE STUDY 2

King IV's five sector supplements recommend the preparation of an integrated report to organisations that may not have been preparing them in the past. The supplements cover: small- and medium-sized enterprises, non-profit organisations, retirement funds, state-owned enterprises and municipalities. At present integrated reports are common practice among South Africa's listed companies and larger state-owned organisations, with some smaller state-owned organisations, municipalities and non-profit organisations also preparing integrated reports.

Integrated thinking extends the consideration by an organisation beyond only financial capital to all forms of capital that are integral to its future success, namely human, intellectual, manufactured, social and relationship, and environmental capital.

 **EXERCISE**

Using these case studies recommend, giving your reasons, the best format for an Annual General Report for an NGO that desperately needs funding. You would need to ensure this report got attention and targeted emotions.

SECTION 3: WRITING SKILLS

CHAPTER 9

RECOGNISING GOOD WRITING

A famous journalist, William Zinsser, wrote: "The secret of good writing is to strip every sentence to its cleanest components."

One of the most famous quotes read to new journalism students: "Don't be tempted by a twenty dollar word when there is a ten-center handy, ready and able!"

Good writing is simple to identify. It's when you can read a document once and come away without any questions on what it's about. If you have to go back and read it a second time it's bad writing.

There's a simple rule here: never write a single word you wouldn't use in everyday conversation. Of course, if you work in a brokerage this means your everyday conversation would be different to someone in the ICT or advertising world.

So why do people deliberately go out of their way to confuse the reader? Simple answer – because they can! Even the Bible says, "Let thy words be few." Not that this means leave out **essential information**. So it all boils down to choosing the right PLAIN words. Use words that:

- Express, not impress
- Convey meaning, not simply show off your extensive vocabulary
- Convey substance

So it's not just writing fewer words but making each word count. Take for instance:

We need to *effectuate improvement* of our training procedures.

Rather write

We need to *improve* our training procedures.

Bad writing:

- Is written in a pompous way with little regard for the reader

- Claims there's no time to get to know the subject matter well

- Blames the reader for not understanding the text received

- Sends off information without any structure or forethought

- Means the reader has to wade through mounds of information before getting the 'message' they need.

Writing without focus

Subject: *Small Business Programme at Zedcom*

Dear Sir,

The Small Business Programme at Zedcom aims to offer all participants the unique opportunity to set up and manage their own business.

All participants will receive essential information on the management and marketing of products, price setting, quality and stock control, and the training of colleagues, as well as learning other management skills.

Zedcom hopes through this initiative to offer participants, at no expense to themselves, increased opportunities, income, and an improved standard of living.

If this programme interests you, information can be obtained by telephoning 0800 0000.

> **Writing with focus**
>
> *ARE YOU SEEKING NEW OPPORTUNITIES, MORE MONEY AND A HIGHER STANDARD OF LIVING?*
>
> *If this is what you are looking for, then take part in the Small Business Programme – a new initiative run by Zedcom.*
>
> *The programme will teach you how to start up and run your own business.*
>
> *You'll learn, in a simple and practical way, how to:*
>
> - manage and market products
> - work out pricing levels
> - improve the quality of products and services
> - control stock
> - train and involve colleagues
>
> *You will also learn basic management skills and techniques.*
>
> *The programme is free of charge, so call 0800 0000 to register your place now.*
>
> *Don't miss out – this is just the opportunity you've been waiting for.*

POMPOUS WRITING

For anyone who wonders if this could actually be real – it is. Taken from a government department document...

> *It has become a matter of mounting importance that we sharpen the spatial focus of government programmes. The macro-framework for this is already in place. The National Spatial Development Perspective (NSDP) has been developed, and was recently updated, with a view to guide us as we seek to direct growth-inducing investment in a coordinated and spatially-targeted way.*

This has implications not only with respect to attracting private sector investments into prioritised geographic spaces, but also with respect to social provision of sustainable modes of living to people who were previously marginalised. This means that we must keep a close watch on our fiscal interventions and the distributional dynamics which are unleashed by these interventions. The test is whether our fiscal interventions, including the way we distribute nationally-raised revenue to local jurisdictions, serve to buttress existing inequalities or they help hitherto marginalised geographic spaces to overcome their inheritance of disadvantage.

Simply put, good writing is simple to identify. It's when you can read a document once and come away without any questions on what it's about. If you have to go back and read it a second time it's bad writing.

USING PLAIN ENGLISH

"I never write metropolis if paid the same amount to write city."
– Mark Twain

Have you ever received something like this?

The purpose of this letter is to provide information you requested regarding whether there is in existence a grace period regarding payment of said medical insurance policy. Please be advised that the aforementioned is of a duration of 10 days following premium due date previously established at the outset of said policy.

What they could have said was:

After the due date, your medical insurance policy allows a 10-day grace period to submit payment.

Again we come back to what writing in this digital world really means – short, to the point and sweet!

There are two very interesting websites that explain the importance and benefits of plain language. Take a look:

Plain language websites:

www.plainenglish.co.uk
www.plainlanguage.gov

**Approved by
Plain English
Campaign**

Each year the Plain English Association gives their 'Crystal-Mark' awards to companies and government organisations who meet their stringent requirements for using plain English. Needless to say not too many organisations qualify!

UNCOMPLICATING COMPLEX WRITING

Good writing is good manners. You can both please and help your public only when you learn how to be the first victim of your writing, how to anticipate a reader's difficulties and to hear yourself as others hear you. – Ritchie R. Ward

 **EXAMPLE – Complaint letter**

From:

Floating Rate Notes: The applicable pricing supplement relating to a floating rate note will designate an interest rate formula for such floating rate note. Such a formula may be the commercial paper rate, in which case such note will be a commercial paper rate; the prime rate, in which case such note will be a prime rate note; the CD rate, in which case such note will be a CD rate note; the federal funds effect rate, in which case such note will be a federal funds effective rate; the Treasury rate, in which case such note will be a Treasury rate note; such other interest rate formula as is set forth in such pricing supplement. The applicable pricing supplement for a floating rate note also will specify the spread and/or spread multiplier, if any, applicable to each note. Any floating rate note may also have either or both of the following: a maximum numerical interest rate limitation, or ceiling or a minimum numerical interest rate limitation, or floor.

To:

Floating Rate Notes

Each floating rate note will have an interest rate formula, which may be based on the:

- *Commercial paper rate*
- *Prime rate*
- *CD rate*
- *Federal funds effective rate*
- *Treasury rate*

> - *Another interest rate*
> - *The applicable pricing supplement will also indicate any spread and/or spread multiplier. In addition any floating rate note may have a maximum or minimum interest rate limitation*

USING NUMBERS/STATISTICS

Would you read this?

Resilient new vehicle market driven by business buying

Despite growth in the commercial segments, total passenger car sales fell 4.4%, year-on-year. Passenger car sales through the dealer channel slumped 5% – a shortfall that could not be counteracted by growth of 26% for passenger cars through the rental channel. Total sales through the rental channel grew 32.5%, year-on-year. Sales through the government channel have also contributed to this month's result – with buying activity in light-, medium- and heavy commercial vehicle segments contributing to growth of 33%

"The growth in the rental channel and commercial vehicle segments is indicative of these businesses entering their replacement cycles, acquiring new assets to refresh their fleets," said xxxxx, Head of Brand and Communications at xxx Bank. "Passenger car sales are still struggling, though. Household budgets remain under pressure and consumers are choosing to hold onto their cars for longer."

Xxx Bank's internal data reflects the trends seen in the consumer space. February saw demand for new vehicles drop 8.4%, year-on-year. Demand for used vehicles also slowed, with 5.3% fewer applications received compared to February last year. Consumers who did finance vehicles also paid more: the average deal value for a new car was 8.8% higher, while the average car was 9% more expensive year-on-year.

"This is the first decline in demand we've seen for used vehicles and we will need more data to see if this is a trend for the year. A number of factors influence this and we will be sure to watch it closely," said xxxx. "However, consumer demand for used vehicles continues to outpace new vehicles by a factor of 2.4:1"

The answer is an obvious no! But if you saw this laid out like this you'd sit up and take note:

Fast Forward

Companies	Jul '15	Jul '16	% Change
Maruti Suzuki	110,405	125,778	13.9
Hyundai India	36,503	41,201	12.9
M&M	14,456	17,356	20
Toyota Kirloskar	12,070	12,404	2.8
Nissan	2,841	6,418	126
Ford	4,362	7,076	62.2
Renault	1,686	11,968	609.8
Honda Cars	18,606	14,033	-24.6

Only domestic sales   Source: Companies

Sales at Hero MotoCorp, the market leader, rose 9.13% to 5,32,113 units in July

At Royal Enfield, sales rose 31% to 53,378.

Another bad example is this release from a pharmaceutical chain announcing their good results over Christmas 2016:

XXX SALES UP 13.6% IN STRONG CHRISTMAS TRADING

Cape Town – Health and beauty retailer Xxxx continued its strong growth momentum in the 20 weeks to mid-January 2017, increasing sales by 13.6%.

Reporting on the Xxxx Group's trading update, chief executive Xxxx said the chain performed well in the current constrained consumer environment, showing volume growth of 4.2%, well ahead of most retailers.

Xxxx increased same store sales by 9.6% with selling price inflation of 5.4%.

Xxxx said customer behaviour continues to reflect a shift to shopping later in the festive season and Xxxx experienced record trading days in the week leading up to Christmas.

"It is most encouraging that we continued to experience buoyant trading in the weeks after Christmas, driven mainly by value promotions across all of our product categories," he said.

Total retail sales for the Group increased by 12.2% and by 8.5% in comparable stores, with selling price inflation averaging 5.3%.

Total group turnover for the 20-week period grew by 8.6% to R10.0 billion. UPD, the group's pharmaceutical wholesale and distribution business, increased turnover by 6.4%, ahead of selling price inflation of 4.3% for the period.

Xxxx said management is confident of maintaining its competitive market position through its value offer to customers and the continued expansion of their stores and pharmacy footprint. "This will be supported by the relative resilience of the health and beauty markets in which we trade," he added.

Again this could look like:

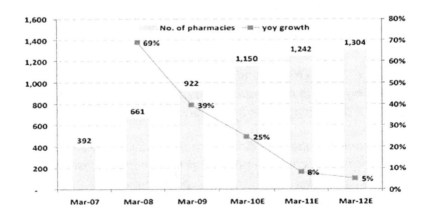

LAYOUT

As mentioned earlier how your document looks is very important. Solid text can put people off. As you will see shortly the definition of a good paragraph is: one thought process/idea – one paragraph.

Where you have various items to list then use bullet points – as I've done all the way through this book. It makes it easier for the reader to digest than solid text.

Italics and bold

Only use italics where necessary to set parts of your text apart and only use bold for headings or to place emphasis on a word/words. If you overuse them they lose their value.

Alignment and indentations

Again, for the sake of the reader, make sure your document is clear and easy to follow by keeping your alignment uniform. In other words, the same margin sizes all the way through and only use indentations where necessary – generally when using bullet points.

Font

This has to be a company decision generally but either Arial 11 or Times Roman 11 are favoured by most companies for this type of writing. Don't try and use fancy fonts as they cloud what you're trying to get across, are often hard to read and don't really add value to a document. Serious writing needs serious fonts.

WRITING IN THE DIGITAL ENVIRONMENT

Tone and style

"Style is the dress of thoughts." – Lord Chesterfield.

"When we come across a natural style, we are surprised and delighted; for we expected an author, and we find a man." – Blaise Pascal

Find your voice....

Tone is a balancing act with words. How often have you heard someone say, 'It's not what he said, but the way he said it. Who does he think he's talking to?' Using the correct tone in your writing or speech is vital for the reader to respond with a positive or open attitude to your message. Tone can also be insulting to some people.

Today, with social media, tone has changed dramatically in many areas. However in most of corporate cases the formal tone is still used. This though shouldn't be confused with plain language.

Style isn't stagnant – it changes and so must your writing.

It doesn't matter whether you're writing a report, email or a newsletter – your aim is to get the reader to read from beginning to end. If you lose them after a line or two you could be in trouble. As a reader you don't want them to think: 'why didn't they just get to the point?' This is at best frustrating. At worst it's such a huge 'turn off' that it can have a negative effect, or even produce an effect that is the exact opposite of the one intended.

Conversational or formal style

This is naturally a style decision within your organisation with some, such as the banking community, being more formal than say a public relations agency. But bear in mind that just because you've been writing in a certain style for the last xxx years doesn't mean that's what's still needed. And if you're currently or have recently been writing for academia then put that right behind you when writing outside the world of papers and theses.

A good test is the following: Ask yourself whether anyone would speak the way you have written. If the answer is no, delete what you've written and start again.

You've always got to take your specific reader's ability or limitations into account – but even if they're a professor of linguistics you still don't need to use long words.

Those of you who have had any journalism training would know you're never just told to write an article or news piece. You're always given a word count. This works well as the journalist then knows they have to get their story across with a firm beginning, middle and end without losing the reader's interest. This goes for all writing and the way to do this is stick to short and sweet... When you look at the following lists many of you will probably find that you use the words on the left more than the right. If so, it's time for a change!

WORDY	CONCISE
accomplish the project	complete, finish
afford an opportunity	allow, permit, enable
attached/enclosed herewith please find	attached, enclosed is/are
at an early date	soon
based on the fact that	because
deem	believe, think, consider
due to the fact that	due to, because
during the time that,	during, when
in addition to the above	also
in close proximity to	near
interpose no objections	agree with
present a conclusion	conclude
with the exception of	except for
take under consideration	consider

Try filling in the column on the right with just one word to replace the three or four on the left.

PADDED	TRIMMED
a large (small) number of	
ahead of schedule	
along the lines of	
at a later date	
draw to your attention	
during the course of	
had occasion to be	
have need for	
in advance of	
in connection with	
in regard (relation) to	
make use of	
not in a position to	
on a regular basis	
on two separate occasions	
put in an appearance	
retain a position as	
take into consideration	
the majority of	
until such time as	

And then you have redundant expressions, which mean you're writing two, three or even four words instead of one. Do any of these sound familiar?

REDUNDANT EXPRESSIONS

AVOID:	INSTEAD, USE:
absolutely nothing	nothing
advance forward	advance
and also	(either word)
assemble together	assemble
at the present time	at present, now
attach together	attach
basic and fundamental	(either word)
but nevertheless	(either word)
close proximity	near
continue on	continue
disappear from sight	disappear

Think about the words you use

Overused and cliched

Language isn't a static thing and with every generation comes new vocabulary, much of which becomes everyday language. Consider all the new terms that have come in with social media alone. Once again, always ask yourself: could I use one word instead of two or more?

INSTEAD OF:	USE:
about-face	reverse
about to	ready
back to square one	begin again
bottom line	main thought
by and large	in general
call on	visit
come up with	create, design
get in touch with	phone, visit, write

INSTEAD OF:	USE:
hand in	submit
keep in mind	remember
wipe out	eliminate
put off	suspend

Jargon

Although you may have to use a certain amount of jargon in your writing, where possible *again* use simple rather than complicated words. Every industry has a certain amount of jargon which is fine within *your* industry – you're all on the same page. BUT if you're writing out of your industry then you have to think hard about the language you use and if necessary give simple explanations.

This might mean supplying background information on a project. Explain the background regarding the setting up and reason behind the project. Include anything that will explain what you're writing about.

Buzzwords

This kind of writing is easy to recognise. Buzzwords sound impressive and convey no real meaning – just what many business people and politicians find useful.

Buzzwords of choice include:

- team
- process
- interactive
- empowerment
- ownership
- strategic
- assessment
- competency
- validate
- asset
- environment
- parameter
- maximise
- focus
- leverage
- system
- paradigm

Combine these randomly and you get meaningless phrases such as:

- "analysis and validation of support strategies for customer satisfaction parameters"
- "maximized systems of strategic environmental processes"
- "parameters of team competency assessment support"
- "focus on ownership of teamwork assessment validation assets"
- "empowering your interactive competency team process"
- "utilising paradigms of support validation strategies of assessment"

Isn't this fun? You too can be 'management material'!

Watch out also for abbreviations and acronyms. If you use either then make sure you put in brackets a full explanation, for instance: ISASA (Independent Schools Association of South Africa).

Headings to grab the reader

In a long document, such as a report, it's essential to 'signpost' what's coming next by using subject and topic headings. This also helps anyone skimming the document for information on a particular part of the document.

It also helps the writer get their thoughts together by using the heading to make sure they just write about that particular point.

The best way to decide on a heading for a document is to get to the heart of the matter. Don't try and be clever – simply use as few words as possible to get to the point of what you're writing.

An effective subject line:

- Attracts your reader's attention
- Provides an accurate, precise description of your subject

EXAMPLE – Complaint letter

Weak subject line:

- *Loading problems*
- *Customer Service*
- *Software Demo Class*

More precise subject line:

- *Container loading problems for vessel* Northern Star *(June 10)*
- *Revised Customer Service Procedures*
- *New accounting software demo class schedule*

EXERCISE

Try and find a heading for the following:

- *A memo on new opening times for the staff canteen to avoid overcrowding and ensuring better service*

- *A letter announcing the new appointment of Charles Gray as Chief Financial Officer who is coming to you from Investec after rising through their ranks from a junior accountant*

- *Your company sells office supplies and you are about to bring out a new robot that will not only clean offices, but do the filing and make coffee*

Introduction of letter/communication

The introductory part of your writing should prepare your readers for what's to come. Put them in the picture by answering these questions:

- What's the subject I'm going to write about?

- Explain the way the document is structured as part of your introduction.

- What particular problem, issues or questions about this am I going to address?

- Why are these issues important?

- What information am I going to introduce to address these issues?

- How am I going to arrange this information to get my point across most clearly?

Don't forget, this is a single paragraph, perhaps even a single sentence. It states the subject or purpose of your letter and acknowledges any previous letter sent by the person you are writing to by quoting its date.

Body – developing and explaining your purpose

If you're writing a long document then, as mentioned previously, you might want to use headings and subheadings to introduce new subjects, so your readers can see immediately when there's a change of topic and what the new subject is.

Once you've written your introduction and the reader knows what the subject matter is, the following applies:

- Tell your readers when you're moving to a new topic.

- Make sure your readers have enough background information to follow your argument. You may find you need to explain some terms briefly or clear up common misconceptions about the topic before you can develop your main theme.

- If you're going to discuss a number of issues, list them all and examine each one separately. This keeps you as well as the readers on track. You may even want to use numbers to separate the points.

- Use tables, lists and diagrams as discussed earlier to present information. Again, use linking devices to join paragraphs.

Main body of letter or email

This should normally be only one or two paragraphs before coming to your conclusion and clearly stating your reason for writing.

 EXAMPLE

Dear

I've seen your recent advertisement on the Internet advertising your expertise in fundraising. We run a home for children affected or infected by HIV/Aids and are in desperate need of funds.

I'd be grateful if you could ring me to set up a meeting to see how we could benefit from your knowledge in this field.

Previous fundraising attempts we've made have simply not worked and as stated above we're in need of funds to simply keep the home open.

Looking forward to hearing from you.

Yours ......

Conclusions

This is generally (as above) a single paragraph which could include recommendations, solutions and calls for action. DON'T introduce new ideas, questions or other information outside the area already covered in your letter/document. Your closing must complete your thoughts; your readers must feel as satisfied with your ending as they would feel with those of a good novel. They must not feel something is missing, unexplained or unexpressed.

 EXAMPLE

Conclusion of report back

Managers agreed that after attending various internal training programmes, participants showed increased confidence, better productivity and improved job performance.

Conclusion of letter

Since I want to display next year's range from early November, I would be grateful if you would give this matter your urgent attention.

Yours.....

Sincerely
Sincerely Yours
Regards
Best Regards
Yours Truly
Respectfully
Thank you

Putting life into your writing

Using the active voice

Simply put, in the active voice the subject of the sentence *does* the action. In the passive voice, the subject is having the action done to it. If you use Windows you can set your spell check to let you know what percentage of your writing is passive (go to Tools to set this).

ACTIVE VOICE	PASSIVE VOICE

Management should consider running courses to improve the staff's writing skills	It is recommended that special attention be paid to how better writing can be achieved through running courses.
Joe Soap wrote the report.	The report was written by Joe Soap.

 EXERCISE

Take the following passive sentences and put them into the active voice.

The presentation was given by Thembi Mogale, a second year student.

Five containers of clothing were shipped to refugees in Ethiopia by the aid agency Gift of the Givers.

A loss of earnings was reported for the year by Crown Mines.

EDITING YOUR WORK

"Read over a passage, and wherever you meet a passage which you think is particularly fine, cross it out." – Samuel Johnson

"I believe more in the scissors than I do in the pencil." – Truman Capote

You've finished typing whatever it is you're writing and you think, 'great, finished' and you send it off – generally at the touch of a button. Wrong. This is a big mistake because it's only in the editing that you're really able to assess whether you've got across the intended message and whether you can make it shorter and easier to read and lastly check for spelling or grammar mistakes. **And no – 'spell check' isn't good enough!**

A good tip, if possible, is to leave what you've just written for a while – for a long document, preferably overnight – returning to it later or the next day to do your edit. You'll generally pick up quite a number of mistakes and feel you can do better.

One of the most important tips I can give you is to **READ YOUR WORK OUT LOUD.** Good writing has a rhythm to it like music. Your writing should flow and not sound awkward. If any part sounds unintelligible, unnecessarily formal, pretentious, or is difficult to read without catching your breath (which means that sentences are too long!) you'll need to change it.

Try breaking up long sentences into shorter ones, each conveying a key point. If possible try and have a break before sending off your work as you'll see it with fresh eyes the second time around and probably find things you missed previously.

A good tip is to put a ruler or envelope under each line to avoid being distracted by the rest of the text.

When you've gone through your work the first time, do it again – this time from the bottom up. It sounds crazy but it works. When you go from the bottom up you're far more likely to find the apostrophe or speech mark you've left out. To be really thorough, a document, such as an article or report, should have four editing processes:

1.   Read aloud to hear your mistakes and flow

2.   Go through the text with a fine tooth comb checking for missing commas, apostrophes etc.

3.   Do a spell and grammar check

4.   Read through slowly to do a final check

 ## Cutting to the quick – taking out unnecessary articles, prepositions and pronouns

Articles (a, an, the), prepositions (of), pronouns (it) and indicative words (there, here) can often be taken out of phrases and sentences where in fact they serve little purpose. Instead of writing 'many of the companies' or 'the use of technology allows', try 'many companies' and 'technology allows'. Rather than 'It was our research department that provided the data', you could state, 'Our research department provided the data.' Economy is the key word here.

A good tip is going through your work and seeing where you can omit the word 'that' – it's one of the most 'cuttable' words in writing.

EXAMPLE

*He said **that** he was very happy **that** he had been promoted to his position in the company. He was sure **that** he would do his best and **that** everything would go well.*

 AN EDITING CHECKLIST

- Is the writing direct to a specific reader?
- Does the writing match what is known about the audience?
- Does the approach take the reader's level of knowledge into account?
- For a lay audience, are terms defined? Examples provided?
- For an audience of experts, are enough supporting facts presented?
- Are conclusions backed up by evidence?
- Do examples help the reader understand?
- Are answers provided for the questions readers are most likely to ask?
- Does the writing have the right tone, the right amount of formality or informality?
- Is the writing bias-free?
- Have you used slanted words, inappropriate labels, or stereotypes?
- Have you given parallel treatment in matters of sex, race, age and ability?

Logic

- Are the ideas clear?
- Was there a plan? Was it followed?
- Is the information coherent?
- Is it presented according to a logical scheme?

Clarity

- Are any words or sentences ambiguous?
- Are antecedents clear? (Will readers understand what words like *it* and *this* refer to?)
- Are words specific rather than vague?
- Do you signal what's coming by such words as *but* or *therefore?*
- Have unintentional double negatives slipped in?

Brevity, conciseness

- Are there too many words?
- Are there redundancies?

Usage

- Do the words convey the desired meaning?
- Are singular and plural words used correctly?
- Are there overworked expressions?
- Do you use the active voice wherever possible?
- Does gobbledygook create a verbal smokescreen?
- Do the words create the right kind of picture?
- Are metaphors effective?
- Are contractions used correctly (especially it's and there's)?

STYLE SHEET

Within your own organisation you should have a style sheet to keep track of decisions within your organisation on such matters as spelling, capitalisation and the treatment of compound words, such as E-Mail, e-mail, email. This is particularly useful when a new member of staff joins your COMPANY.

 EXAMPLE

Acronyms

The acronym for a phrase, product or company is always written in brackets **after** the phrase, e.g. the Automobile Association (AA). Repeat the acronym in place of the full name for the rest of the story.

Only insert the acronym if it is used again in the story or in the headline, otherwise leave it out because it is UNNECESSARY!

Use only capital letters in acronyms, not a mixture of upper and lower case, e.g. it is VOIP not VoIP (the latter is an Americanism).

Do not use full stops in acronyms.

Avoid an acronym 'soup' (too many acronyms directly after each other).

Where the acronym forms a pronounceable word (e.g. Unix) use upper and lower case.

Where the acronym does not form a pronounceable word (e.g. PABX) use upper case only.

Americanisms

Watch out for American slang and Zs!

Some words have a different meaning in SA and America. For example, 'slated' in the US means expected or scheduled (e.g. the product is slated for release in June). In SA it means to criticise severely (e.g. analysts have slated the new move).

Zs:	Double Ls:
organisation (NOT organization) The same goes for: criticise revolutionise popularise analysed globalise stabilised centralised	totalling labelling dialling fuelling (US uses one L)

Also, it is colour and labour, NOT color and labor; also it's grey not gray.

 **EXERCISES**

Email Exercise

The purpose of this email is to inform you that the Maintenance Department will begin work on the following list of various outdoor repairs on June 28 but you need to know that all this depends on the weather because as you know it has been a wet month. So it is important to bear in mind that the following list of repairs may not be completed as scheduled for July 10.

Write two short sentences to explain this clearly.

| |
| |
| |

Letter Exercise

Dear Sir,

Thank you for your letter regarding the extremely bad service you received from our company. Whilst we fully understand your frustration with solving this particularly difficult, complex, problem we have to explain why our call centre staff member was apparently unable to help you at the time. When he tried to locate your records he encountered a problem with your subscription number. It appears that this number was in fact allocated, at different times, to different people, none of whom appears to be yourself. What we would like you to do now is to please send us your original correspondence showing this number in print with your personal details. In this way we can then attempt to rectify this most unfortunate situation.

Yours.....

1. Shorten this in plain, simple language.

2. Try and rewrite the following in a more concise way:

    a. *During the year 2017*

    b. *Fines were applied in line with the relevant regulations*

    c. *We wish to make the most of this opportunity to inform you*

| |
| |
| |

CHAPTER 10

WRITING IN DIGITAL ENVIRONMENTS

Whether you're writing for a website, marketing channel, social media or a promotional brochure there are certain key factors that remain the same. In fact all the way through this book the same message comes through – that whatever you write the idea is to keep your audience reading. In the case of digital this means not clicking off the page.

So how do you 'hook' your audience and keep them engrossed?

When I was researching this chapter I found it easy to find long boring releases on company websites but really battled to find good, short and to-the-point ones. None of the major food/retail outlets, banks or building societies yielded even one halfway decent news piece/release.

What most people want to know is: what are the fundamental differences between writing for 'print' as against 'digital'? In a nutshell, research shows the biggest change in people's reading habits come from the constant bombardment of information we get daily. From the moment you wake up you're reading your mobile phone, tablet and computer, checking out your emails, Facebook, Twitter, favourite news sites and so on. This goes on throughout the day with the brain taking in small snippets of whatever it decides is important.

The answer then is to understand these habits and utilise this knowledge to make sure you grab and hold your readers.

HOW DO READERS SEE DIGITAL CONTENT?

Research shows that instead of reading word for word and line for line readers see digital content page by page – in other words visually. Here are some examples of press releases. See which you would read and those you'd give a miss to.

X company introduces xxxxxx – a symbol of luxury for a new era

*Rarely, a brand releases an offering so exceptional and **unique** that the world – typically busy to the point of obliviousness – stops to consider the prestige and pleasure that owning such a singular treasure would bring.*

*Clive Christian No. 1 Perfume, 'heart-made' Patchi chocolates, diamond-encrusted teabags by PG Tips, the Baldi-Harrods crystal bathtub, Stuart Weitzman's ruby slippers…all of these items are so **unique** and highly valued not only because of the prized and at times scarce resources needed for their creation, but also for the incomparable craftsmanship that took the mundane and transformed it into art. Now, the latest edition to this prestige list is xxxx's the xxxxxxxxxxxx*

Blended and perfected by Master blender Joe Soap, this limited edition scotch offers connoisseurs a taste of the brand's rich, *century long history; with every luscious, sweet yet smoky sip, the drinker can discern the **unique** but balanced and complementary flavours of each hand-selected malt sourced to create the scotch, some originating from Highland distilleries that are now lost forever.*

"Xxxx is the pinnacle of a prestige brand that has lasted for more than one hundred years," says brand manager Wordy McWord. "It is a symbol of exclusivity and sumptuous luxury for a new era. However, xxxx also represents attainable luxury, along with selectivity. Our range presents a number of whiskeys to suit different budgets, offering South Africans an experience of refined opulence."

To further the impression and sensation of high sophistication, The xxxx is presented in a hand-blown crystal decanter created by xxxx Crystal – the only major crystal producer in the UK and a manufacturer often lauded for the style and quality of their creations. The glass is delicately engraved and refined with crafted metalwork and presented in magnificent green glassware in honour of the original xxxx bottle that first captured the world's attention in the early 20th century. The bottle is further embellished with a signature stopper, a Celtic symbol of love.

Xxxx is a truly exquisite blend – perfectly smooth with an intense concentration of sumptuous flavours that develop into an exceptionally long, lingering finish," says Mr McWord. "I am proud to present this luxurious expression of the xxxx house style to you."

A side note to mention here is that the word ***unique*** when writing press releases is a red rag to a raging journalist… Don't ever, ever use it.

The DTI Media Statement: Fuel Cell Bus Workshop Whets Appetite of SA Cities[2]

---

2   The DTI Media Statement. February, 2017. Fuel Cell Bus Workshop Whets Appetite of SA Cities. Retrieved from: https://www.thedti.gov.za/editmedia.jsp?id=3965

*The fuel cell bus workshop that was hosted by the Department of Trade and Industry (**the dti**) in partnership with the German government in Cape Town has stimulated a lot of interest amongst South African cities to introduce buses powered by hydrogen/ platinum fuel cells on their roads.*

The purpose of the workshop, which was held under the theme 'Fuel Cell Bus – Unleashing Industrial Opportunities for South Africa through a Zero Emission Choice', was to provide a platform where South Africa can learn from the Germans who successfully rolled out fuel cell buses in various cities.

"The knowledge and information that the Germans shared with us really created a lot of interest among delegates from both the private sector and government in general, and representatives of our metropolitan cities in particular.

As government we will be harnessing the enthusiasm and energy that was generated by the workshop to chart the way forward as part of our fuel cell roadmap. The dti will be working in collaboration with the Departments of Environmental Affairs and Science and Technology to lead the process and provide assistance. We will all be happy if we can launch a fuel cell bus in the country in twelve to eighteen months even if it is for demonstration purpose," said the Chief Director of Primary Mineral Processing at the dti, Mr Tapiwa Samanga.

He added that the dti was impressed with the response that the workshop received as it showed that various stakeholders are keen to take advantage of opportunities the fuel cell industry presents. Key stakeholders in the SA bus transportation and mining industries attended the workshop; these include Platinum Group Metals mining companies, bus manufacturers as well as officials from various departments and metros.

"We are not leaving anybody outside as we would want to take advantage of the whole fuel cell value chain. A lot of work still has to be done until somebody deploys a fuel cell demo bus on our roads. And thereafter someone has to buy them. The interest

shown by the cities in procuring these buses will undoubtedly stimulate their development. It will be all hands on deck going forward until we achieve our objective," added Samanga.

He said South Africans learnt from the Germans that an integrated planning approach will mitigate the high development costs. The Germans had started with a piece-meal approach and that raised the development costs; SA cannot afford to make the same mistakes.

"As government we are looking beyond just using fuel cells in buses. We are casting our vision wider and will look broadly at fuel cells as contributing to the country's energy mix, cleaner energy, mineral beneficiation, job creation, economic growth and transformation, as well as earning export revenue," said Samanga.

Bridging the distance in distance education[3]

Unisa's Department of Communication Science is taking distance education teaching to an all new high having introduced interactive live broadcast classes to its students. Channelling new frontiers in digital teaching, the department has been using numerous communication tools for teaching purposes.

From the use of blogs, Twitter, satellite broadcasting, video conferencing and Skype, among others, the department now uses Open Broadcasting Software with live streaming from YouTube, and, more recently, Google Hangouts to bring the theory alive for their students.

Prof Danie du Plessis, who began using Google Hangouts late in 2016, said for too long, because of Unisa's distance education methodologies, students have been isolated with impersonal material as resources. The aim, he said, is to provide large numbers of students with interactive classes that allow them to engage and influence the lecture and lecturer and other students.

---

3   Naidu-Hoffmeester, R., & Hanekom, J. (nd). Bridging the distance in distance education. Unisa News & Media. Retrieved from: http://www.unisa.ac.za/sites/corporate/default/ News-&-Media/Articles/Bridging-the-distance-in-distance-education

Presenting the concept of Google Hangouts at a College of Human Sciences board meeting, Du Plessis said that Unisa's purpose is to educate and skill people who will make a difference and change the world.

"Our teaching, research, and community engagement should all focus on making an impact and addressing real problems. By solving these problems we can have real impact. When we empower our students, thousands of them over a long time, with the skills, values and attitudes to tackle problems in our communities and society, we will make a difference in the world of individual students. By empowering students that will contribute to better communities and society we can have a positive impact on the world and make it a better place to live in."

Optimising teaching efforts

He said through the ages the main concern with distance education was the fact that there was no direct contact with students, so, in an attempt to optimise efforts, they began using various communication tools such as blogs, Twitter, satellite broadcasting, video conferencing, and Skype, among others, all of which form part of their department's Digital Teaching Lab (DTL).

The most commonly used teaching tool is the Open Broadcasting Software (OBS) with live streaming from YouTube. A link is generated using JoinIn Application, which works in conjunction with OBS, and then shared with the students. The link takes students to a page that will grant them access to the live video broadcast stream. In this live stream, students are able to navigate different parts such as the Q&A section, which allows them to ask questions and also vote for them to make them high priority to the lecturer. At the same time, students are able to pause, rewind and forward during the live stream.

In addition to this method of teaching, Google Hangouts, because of its ability to reach a much larger group of students, is also becoming a tool of choice. According to Google, Google

Hangouts is a unified communications service that allows members to initiate and participate in text, voice or video chats, either one-on-one or in a group. Hangouts are built into Google+ and Gmail, and mobile Hangouts apps are available for iOS and Android devices. This means that Unisa students can participate in these classes where ever they are located, as long as they have access to data, Wi-Fi and a smart phone.

Du Plessis said given the reach they could have with Google Hangouts, they collaborated with Google, Grove (Google premium partners) and developed the concept further by simplifying and enhancing the broadcasting process, interface, and the question-and-answer function.

"The result is that class can be attended from any device and from anywhere live or at any time, students attending a live class have the opportunity to ask questions, comment and influence the lecturer and lecture by using the tools, and students who could not attend live can also watch the broadcast afterwards and still join the discussion in the question-and-answer session, which will stay live if so preferred by the lecturer."

First-year students experience it for themselves

Since they began using Google Hangouts, Du Plessis has done six live broadcasts for module COM3708, which saw an increase in the pass rate from 55 percent in the first semester to 76 percent in the second.

All first-time undergraduate students who are registered for formal qualifications experienced this tool on 20 February 2017 when they were invited to join a live session by accessing it from any smart device. The invitation was sent out to 61 457 students, some of whom joined the live session while others watched it later.

They were addressed by Prof Gugu Moche, Vice-Principal of Teaching, Learning, Community Engagement, and Student Support, and her academic and student support team, Prof

Peter Havenga, Prof Oupa Mashile, and Dr Matome Mashiapata. During the live interactive session, the presenters explained to students on how to survive at Unisa and how to be successful in their studies.

The students also had the opportunity to provide feedback, ask questions, and complete a short online survey regarding the value of the event. The survey revealed that 82.8% of the students thought that the live broadcast was useful, 92.1% indicated that they would like to see more similar broadcasts in future and 95.8% indicated that they would like to see live broadcasts used for teaching modules.

Moche and her team explained that, since Unisa is a distance education institution, studying at the university might at first be an overwhelming experience as distance education required unique skills, attitudes, and learning approaches.

The team assured the students that Unisa is committed to bridging the distance in distance education. Havenga explained the open, distance, and e-learning (ODeL) environment, while Mashile and Mashiapata explained student and staff management systems and emphasised the numerous student support systems available.

CITY OF EKURHULENI[4]

Ekurhuleni
METROPOLITAN MUNICIPALITY

---

4   Makhumbila, J. 3 March 2017. Free Bicycles for Primary School Learners. City of Ekurhuleni. Retrieved from: https://www.ekurhuleni.gov.za/yourservices/news/press-releases/free-bicycles-for-primary-school-learners

Walking long distances to and from school will soon be a thing of the past for some learners of Umnyezane Primary School in Putfontein, Benoni.

The City of Ekurhuleni, in partnership with Gauteng Department of Roads and Transport and Gauteng Department of Education, will tomorrow, March 3, 2017, hand out over 100 bicycles to learners through the Shova Kalula programme.

Details of the Shova Kalula bicycles handover ceremony are as follows:

Date: *Friday, March 3, 2017*
Time: *12:00*
Venue: *Umnyezane Primary School (Putfontein)*

Daredevil Run collects R500,00 for CANSA[5]

At least 3,402 men stripped down to their purple Speedos to participate in this year's Hollard Daredevil Run which was held in Johannesburg, Cape Town, Durban, and Mbombela.

---

5 Bizcommunity.com. 29 March 2017. *Daredevil Run collects R500,000 for CANSA.* Retrieved from: http://www.bizcommunity.com/Gallery/196/40/4281.html.html

The event is held in an effort to raise male cancer awareness and this year's event raked up nearly R500,000 for The Cancer Association of South Africa.

#Bookmarks2017: Digital download with ... Honeykome[6]

Local digirati shone at the recent IAB Bookmark Awards 2017. Here's digital feedback from Honeykome's creative director Gordon Laws and art director Allan Slow. March 29th, 2017.

The winning team, L to R: Allan Slow, art direction; Michael Walker, media strategist; Desere Orrill, MD; Leeroy Duke, client services; Ryan Jonathan, animation. In absence: Gordon Laws, creative director; Jacob Claassens, videographer; Slade Reyneke, media buyer.

Honeykome was presented with an 'innovative use of media' bronze pixel for online sports betting site Sportingbet's I Bet You Don't Skip at the Bookmark Awards.

 That's why the team sent through this thumbs up emoji to show how they're currently feeling.

"Every year the calibre of work gets set a little higher. This year was no different with fantastic examples of work from a wide variety of brands, agencies and publishers. We shone in the category of innovative use of media, winning a bronze," say Laws and Slow, with credit for the work also going to their video editing team and their performance media buying team."

---

6   Andrews, L. 29 March 2017. #Bookmarks2017: Digital download with ... Honeykome. Bizcommunity. Retrieved from: http://www.bizcommunity.com/Article/196/459/159708. html

Click here for the full list of 2017 IAB Bookmarks Award winners and visit our special section for the latest updates.

The first three examples are old-fashioned text-heavy pieces – totally unsuitable for digital media yet are on these organisation's websites.

The second three examples are visually pleasing and light on text with the effect that you can take in the message easily and quickly.

This is called the **SKIM FACTOR**! So, is there a specific amount of content that's just right?

Quick answer – no. It varies completely from person to person. Yes, some people definitely will just look at the pictures and captions, others will skim the content and some will definitely read every word on the page – as long as there aren't too many…

So how do you know who to write to? Well, the good news is you don't have to. You can create content that's meant to be read, half read/half ignored (skimmed).

When you create content to be skimmed you're probably catering for each type of audience who will then take away what they need, ignoring the rest.

Skimmers and scanners vs longer readers

To quote Steve Jobs '…the fact is people don't read anymore' – meaning they prefer to do it online. Which brings us to the question: Do people really read online content or are they scanning?

Non-readers

Definitely won't read lengthy text. They want small bites of content (short product descriptions, photos with captions or Twitterbites. They don't want multi-paragraph-learn-all-about-how-great-our-stuff-is sales spiel.

They'll go from page to page until they find what they're looking for. The page will speak to them, not the words. They want to 'get it' straight away without having to read unnecessary words.

This doesn't mean design pages just with pictures. What it means is that all content is non-obtrusive and doesn't stop the non-reader's search and navigation experience. They can look at the page and pluck what they want from it.

Readers

There are still people who will read almost every word on a page – they're generally information buffs. They want details – about a product, a company, an event and its virtues to be convinced they're making the right decision about their purchase.

For these few readers all information is generally good information. But this doesn't mean it should be solid blocks of text. It still has to be written as concisely and crisply as possible with links to categories and sub-categories if necessary.

Skimmers

They skim through a page looking for quick visual cues to help them get the information they want. When they find this they'll generally stop and read more thoroughly or click a link to get to the content they want.

Content written for skimmers helps *all* visitors get a feel of what you're saying/selling without reading every word. Skimmable content helps a reader and non-reader get to where they want to be without reading every word.

For readers it enhances a page and at the same time doesn't get in the way of non-readers. In fact, because it's easy to look at with eye-catching info, the non-reader should find it almost irresistible.

The award for a really bad press release has however to go to Cell C who, when announcing Miss South Africa 2017, published on their website a 414-word release WITHOUT A SINGLE PHOTO OF THIS LADY!!!

WEB USABILITY RESEARCH

Jakob Nielsen, who heads up the Nielsen Norman Group, has been called the guru and king of Web page usability and the following comes from his research:

- Web users spend **80% of their time** looking at information **above the page fold** (meaning the part of the webpage users first land on). Although users do scroll they allocate only 20% of their attention below the fold.

- Users spend 69% of their time looking at the **left half of the webpage** and 30% viewing the right half.

- Visitors decide whether to stay on a page within the first 10 seconds.

- If they're interested enough to stay for 30 seconds they may stay longer – at least two minutes or more. Which, in Web content time, is a big deal.

So what this means is that every word you write and every graphic you use has to have impact. There can be no padding or unnecessary words – anything that will make the user click off.

Understand your traffic

Knowing what your visitors want is crucial to the success of your site. Make sure you use a good traffic analysis programme like Google Analytics, Statcounter etc. You need to know:

- What search terms do visitors use the most to find your site? What do the people searching for these terms want? Do they get it here?

- What are the least popular search terms used to find your site? Does your site rank high for any of these terms? Why are these terms still unpopular then?

- What path do they follow on your site? Can you guess where they want to go? Are they getting there with relative ease?

In my case it's 'Media, Consulting, Training, Journalism, Writing, Editing, and Ghost Writing'.

THE IMPORTANCE OF MOBILE USAGE

What do you see when you're:

- In a taxi
- A train
- Sports stadium
- Movie house
- Restaurant

You see people on mobile phones, more often than not on their search engines, scouring the net for information, making mobile the first port of call for seeking information.

How often have you been somewhere when someone will ask a question that requires an instant answer – Google to the rescue. What this means is with this increased usage of mobile, particularly Smartphones, content has to be designed with this in mind.

In other words content has to span all channels with the message, look and ethos of your brand staying constant across all three or four mediums.

Again, Neilsen research shows that it's 108% harder to understand information when reading from a mobile screen. They also found users are generally rushed when using mobile devices with less patience to navigate. Bottom line is – **short is too long** for mobile. Ultra-short is the golden rule!

YOU CAN'T JUST PUT YOUR WEBSITE ON YOUR MOBISITE – TWO DIFFERENT THINGS!!!

It's suggested that instead of trying to get all the information on to one screen, secondary or slightly less important information should be used on secondary screens. The first screen users see should be ruthlessly focused on the minimum information needed to communicate your top point.

EXAMPLE - Shutterfly

Shutterfly is an online service that allows users to create photo books, personalised cards, stationery, and more. Because more and more people are taking photos and then accessing them using their smartphones, Shutterfly recognised the need to create a great mobile experience for their customers – and they delivered.

Shutterfly accomplishes two key goals on their mobile website:

- It's easy for users to find out information about their offerings.

- They're selling that information by way of beautiful imagery.

When you arrive on their mobile site, you'll see the menu items have been enhanced into large buttons at the bottom half of the screen. This makes it easy for users to quickly select which option they're interested in learning more about.

Once users click through to one of those options, they're greeted with large photos showcasing what Shutterfly is capable of for easy browsing.

EXAMPLE – Etsy

Etsy is an ecommerce website where people can buy and sell vintage or handmade items. Most buyers who visit Etsy's website are there to do one of two things: Either they're searching for a specific item, or they're browsing items in categories that interest them.

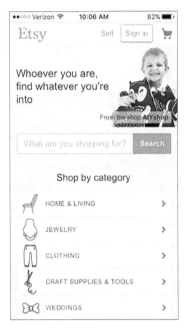

The mobile website caters to both types of visitors from the very beginning. When you first go to their mobile website, you're greeted with an option to search for specific items, shops, or categories.

Immediately below the search bar are thumbnail images of trending items that showcase some of the most popular things you can buy on Etsy. Mobile users can view these trending items in a collage format, and the images are big enough for them to easily tap with their finger.

Dreadful mobi site

The most obvious difference when writing for a website and a mobile is the size and readability of the page. First thing is to test a website on a mobile device and see how easy it is to navigate your way around.

The same rule applies in terms of 'managability and readability' as on any site – with more challenges. Chief content rule again – **KEEP IT SHORT AND TO THE POINT.**

Don't assume one site fits all. It's important to understand what people want on a mobile site. People on mobile phones want information even quicker than a standard web page.

Once you know their needs make sure the user experience is a hassle-free one.

Smartphones today can display most websites and pages but remember:

- On a small screen too many columns are hard to read without zooming

- One column is far better

- Put lists in a logical order for speed

- Put short logical links at the end of every section to relevant content so users don't waste time entering text into search boxes

- Divide pages into smaller chunks. Again, long text-heavy pages just won't work. Snippets are the answer

- Keep URLs short – no room for long ones

- Web pages designed for mobiles should clearly show the content and headline

- Keep your images small and easily downloadable

- Don't put large images at the top of your page – they take too long to open and by then the reader's clicked off

- Be ruthless in cutting out unnecessary words without losing the reader's interest

- Don't bother with a home page welcoming them to the site

- Leave space between links so fingers can navigate easily

The digital mind-frame

"To get the right word in the right place is a rare achievement. To condense the diffused light of a page of thought into the luminous flash of a single sentence, is worthy to rank as a prize composition just by itself... Anybody can have ideas – the difficulty is to express them without squandering a quire of paper on an idea that ought to be reduced to one glittering paragraph."

– Letter to Emeline Beach, 10 Feb 1868

To get into the digital mind-frame there are certain 'rules' to learn and possibly styles to change.

Bearing in mind the golden digital rule of keeping it short and sweet, here are some current stats on readership of websites:

- 10 163 page views (17%) that lasted less than 4 seconds. In such brief 'visits' users clearly bounced right out without truly 'using' the page.

- 2 615 page views (4%) that lasted more than 10 minutes. In these cases, users almost certainly left the browser open while doing something else.

- 1 558 page views (3%) with fewer than 20 words on them. Such pages are probably server errors or disrupted downloads.

Unless people are researching academic papers they generally only read about 5–10% of a page's text.

Obviously, users tend to spend more time on pages with more information. However, the best-fit formula tells us that they spend only **4.4 seconds more for each additional 100 words**.

Don't bother with long introductions. People want really short blurbs, not 'welcome to our new, improved site – we really think you will enjoy this and......'

Remember, generally people go to a site to get what they want and get out – not for a reading session.

Less is more. So even when you think you've cut a paragraph down to the bare bones, go through it again and see how much shorter you can make it.

WRITING TIPS FOR ONLINE WRITING

Use short sentences

- One subject – one sentence
- Uncomplicate complicated text or figures
- Where you have sets of figures use graphs
- Keep sentences on average to 15 or less words

Seconds count!

- First 11 characters of a page title are most important
- People decide in five seconds if your site is useful
- Divide information into small clear pieces (chunk content)

Use headings to cluster or chunk similar content (great with similar or related topics)

- Remember, your web content is a conversation with the consumer. If material doesn't belong in the conversation, it doesn't belong on the web
- Research what your customers really want
- You aren't Santa Claus. You can't serve everyone

They don't necessarily need to know:

- When your company was formed
- Who is the head
- What the head said the day he was sworn in
- What the head looks like
- What your annual report from three years ago looked like
- How the company is organised
- What you did for customers five years ago

They do need:

- Answers to likely questions in easy-to-navigate format
- Informative headings to help navigate
- Increased white space on the page to break up information

Question headings:

- Help readers relate to information
- Help you organise information – using lists
- Make it easy for the reader to identify all items or steps in a process
- Use numbers for steps in process, bullets for everything else

Help the reader see how you've structured your document. Make it clear what readers have to do:

- Make sure items in a list match
- Use command voice (second person)
- Put the verb first
- Get to the point
- Keep your bullets short – use short paragraphs
- Limit a paragraph to one subject or step
- Smaller 'bites' of info are easier to digest
- Aim for no more than seven lines per paragraph/point
- Refer to your organisation as 'we'
- Refer to the reader as 'you' in the text and as 'I' in questions
- Don't use 'he/she' or 'his/her'

EXAMPLE - Etsy

Wrong

1. Copies of tax returns must be provided

2. Loan applications will be reviewed to ensure that procedures have been followed

3. The applicant will be the primary source of information regarding his or her circumstances for the purposes of determining eligibility and need

Correct

1. **You** must provide copies of tax returns

2. **We** will review loan applications to ensure you have followed procedures

3. **You** will be the primary source of information regarding your circumstances for determining your eligibility and need

EXERCISE

Try these:

1. To confirm booking identification a credit card must be brought to the ticket office

2. If this is not done in three days tickets will be forfeited

3. The tickets cannot be retrieved by any third party

When this doesn't work

•   If you're addressing more than one audience

- If you refer readers to more than one office within your organisation

One short paragraph – one idea

This means site visitors can:

- Easily scan each paragraph

- Get the general gist of what the paragraph is about

- Then move on to the next paragraph

All this **without fear they'll be skipping over important information**, because they'll already know roughly what the paragraph is about.

Limiting each paragraph to just one idea is especially effective when combined with front-loading paragraph content.

Front-loading content

This simply means **putting the conclusion first**, followed by the what, who, how, where, when and why. The first line of each paragraph should contain the conclusion for that paragraph, so site visitors can:

- Quickly scan through the opening sentence

- Instantly understand what the paragraph is about

- Decide if they want to read the rest of the paragraph or not

Because each paragraph contains just one idea, users can do all this, safe in the knowledge that if they jump to the next paragraph they won't be missing any new concepts.

Front-loading also **applies to web pages**, as well as paragraphs. The opening paragraph on every page should always contain the conclusion of that page. This way, site visitors can understand what the page is about and decide whether they want to read the page or not.

A big mistake many websites make is writing page content in story-format. This is where any journalistic skills you have may not work.

Each page must have an introduction, middle and conclusion, in that order. Unfortunately, because scanning web content often means we don't read all the text or read to the bottom of the screen, it's easy to miss the conclusion if it's left until the end.

So remember, **conclusion first**, everything else second!

Use descriptive sub-headings

Breaking up text with descriptive sub-headings makes it easy for site visitors to **see what each section of the page is about**. The main heading on the page provides a brief overall view of what the page is about, and the opening paragraph gives a brief conclusion of the page (because you've front-loaded the page content). Within the page though, there are various sub-themes that can be quickly put across with sub-headings.

There's no hard-and-fast rule for **how frequently to use sub-headings**, but you should probably be aiming for one sub-heading every two to four paragraphs. More importantly, the sub-headings should group on-page content into logical groups to allow easy access to the information they're after. This can be in boxes or cloud form or whatever.

IMPORTANCE OF KEY WORDS AND PHRASES – SEO'S

The idea of keywords is to help drive traffic to your site. In other words, if your business is selling carpets, what wording will make your site come up on the first page? Put simply, they are words search engines look for to profile and index websites. They tell search engines what a website is about. Google however keep changing their algorithms and some people feel keywords are becoming less important. But it doesn't hurt to use them for now – I've found them very important.

Having said that, there's more to it than simply sticking keywords onto a page x amount of times.

USEFUL TIPS

- Research popular keyword phrases for your niche. Find a keyword research tool – some are free, others charge

- Write down all the keyword phrases you want to use in your articles and then create article topics or titles for each set of keywords

- Decide on the density needed for each article. I use three keywords per piece – some people use up to five when writing a 500-word article

- Again, the shorter the better but be careful that by using keywords your article still makes sense

- Always double check your copy – not just a spell check to make sure there are no mistakes. As stated in previous chapters read what you've written aloud. The minute people see silly mistakes on your site they won't take it seriously.

- The real prize is if you can come up with a phrase that will tick a few boxes and be used as individual words – '*Best performing financial results for brokerage*'

- If you can use single words or short phrases that are parts of queries you could also get extra rankings

- BEFORE you start writing with SEO in mind find the words you need and make a list and then check at the end if they're all there

  - Use a dictionary, Thesaurus, Wikipedia, etc.

  - Don't just use nouns, use verbs, adverbs and adjectives also

  - Where possible get keywords into your title tag unless this means having an unreadable headline

The bottom line is to remember SEO writing is about writing keyword-optimised copy which is READABLE and persuades visitors to take action. There's a big difference between writing SEO-optimised copy and keyword stuffing. Write optimised copy.

CHECKLIST FOR EFFECTIVE WEB WRITING

Use lists

Lists are preferable to long paragraphs because they:

- Allow users to read the information vertically rather than horizontally
- Are easier to scan
- Are less intimidating
- Are usually more succinct

Left-align text

Left-aligned text is easier to read than justified text, which in turn is easier to read than centre or right-aligned text.

When reading through justified text the spacing between each word is different so our eyes have to search for the next word. This slows down our reading speed. Right- and centre-aligned paragraphs slow down reading speed even more because each time you finish reading one line your eye has to search for the beginning of the next line.

Graphics and pictures

We're all big kids really and want to see pictures to show us what you mean or are offering, so illustrate as much as possible. If you want me to come to your art gallery opening give me a glimpse of what's on show. If you want me to come to your restaurant show me the food and make my mouth water.

Style

Once you've established your style of writing, stick to it. It looks strange on a website when the style varies.

Firstly, remember who you're writing for – not for yourself, but for Joe and Lerato out there. Generally, Joe and Lerato don't know you, and are not particularly interested in you. They're looking for information. Write your pages to deliver what the reader wants. Avoid me-centric phrasing. Take yourself right out of the picture. Tell your reader what they want to know.

Know your USP – unique selling position

Anyone visiting your page must immediately know what you do. If they're confused they'll leave the page immediately.

Stress the benefits

Most people visiting your site ask "what's in it for me?" Therefore provide the main benefits of your products or services within the first few paragraphs. Don't make the mistake of emphasising features instead of benefits.

Be specific

Writing in general terms will only bore your visitors. Instead focus your writing on making specific points. It will help keep your readers focused.

Use bullet points

If you have several points to make in a paragraph, use bullet points. It will make it easier to read by drawing attention to these points.

Include action verbs

Use action verbs at the beginning of your sentences to grab your reader's attention. Examples of action verbs include: discover, how, get, etc. Another way to get readers' attention is by asking questions i.e. "Are you getting a lot of website traffic but not generating any sales?"

Use white space

A cluttered web page is very difficult to read. Make sure you include plenty of white space between all elements on the page. For example, add 5 to 10 pixels of white space between an image and the content.

WRITING ENGAGING COPY

If you were looking for a retirement annuity or adopting a new pet the first place you'd go would be online. Which of these appeals to you?

Retirement planning *is key if you want to enjoy your retirement. Retirement planning consists of two phases:* ***pre-retirement*** *funding and* ***post-retirement income****. Pre-retirement funding means investing in a* ***retirement annuity****. Things to consider include how much you can currently afford to invest and how long you have until you reach retirement age. The second phase –* ***post-retirement income*** *– requires investing the proceeds of your retirement annuity into a life or* ***living annuity****. Post-retirement income considerations include choosing a product that is able to sustain capital growth while you receive an income and regularity of income payments.*

OR

Retirement Annuities

Due to the effects of inflation, most of us will barely survive on our retirement money. Unless we protect both our capital and returns which is what a retirement annuity can do for you.

Apart from the tax advantages you get on your contributions, portfolio growth and your final pay-out, a retirement annuity also offers other great features and benefits:

- A large range of possible investment funds
- The flexibility to invest in more than one investment fund at a time
- A choice of multiple investment funds
- The flexibility to switch between them at any time

- The flexibility to inject extra lump sums over and above your monthly contributions or lump-sum investment

- Continuing your contributions if you change jobs, and

- A choice of pension plans when you retire

What will work and where

It's not just about words – in fact it's far from it. Here are a few tips to think about to make your site more user-friendly:

- Add videos (YouTube or your own) – makes your text come alive – max 1.30 secs.

- Use slides, animation and live action. They can either go at the end of your text or in between.

- Add photos – if you don't want to go with video, photos can help get your message home. Instead of telling people about your CSI work, show them a photo of your team in action helping other people.

- Add podcast – do an interview where a key person is then shown on screen giving their story. This can be someone who's benefited from your services just as well as the head of the organisation.

Secret here – keep it short – three to five minutes…

- Add a blog.

- Add a Facebook 'Like' button – with over 1.26 billion users you could tap into that massive community.

- Share your content on Twitter – again with about a billion users this can't be ignored.

CHAPTER 11

YOUR BRAND ON SOCIAL MEDIA

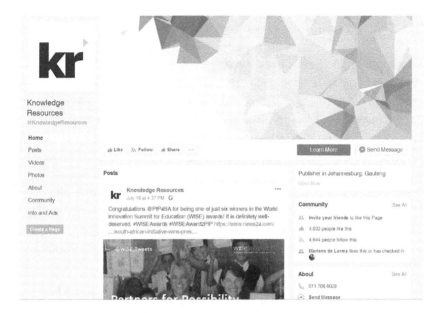

SOCIAL MEDIA AND COMMUNICATION

First we need to look at what people use social media for – to keep up with family and friends, share photos and news. Not generally to see advertisements or sales pitches. If they feel they're being marketed to, then you could end up being ignored, or worse, blocked.

First rule to remember is that social media users are more likely to respond to ads that interact with a reader on a person-to-person level, rather than an advertiser-consumer relationship.

Social media is all about having two-way conversations. This can be with humour, sarcasm, photos, trivia or 'your choice'. Your method though has to fit your brand and at the same time be as creative as possible. THINK WAY OUTSIDE THE BOX!

You need to reinvent your brand to be something that **consumers want to *talk* to.** This is the single most important skill the web copywriter has in terms of reaching the social media community. If your content isn't immediately approachable and interactive you're not going to make it.

Speak on a one-to-one level

Your social voice needs to be even more conversational than ever. Write as if you were speaking to a single individual rather than a demographic or group of people. Rather than saying 'IcyCool Ice Cream makes your summer rich and creamy', rather write 'Visiting the in-laws this summer? Stash some IcyCool Ice Cream to make the visit less painful.' This type of posting taps into the social media mindset.

Social media users see their feeds as the place to vent frustrations, announce successes and tell everyone about their daily happenings. Tapping into something as universal as dreading a trip to the in-laws strikes just the right chord in social media – and it's great copywriting.

Post with a purpose

In social media copywriting every post is important and an opportunity for interaction. Look at every Tweet, photo, and status update and ask: what do we want the reader to do with this? WHY WOULD SOMEONE SHARE THIS? Every brand's voice is different – some lend themselves to fun and some are more factual. Ultimately your audience will decide when you see whether and what they're sharing.

Don't always expect big numbers

Social media copywriting still doesn't share the reach traditional advertising methods do. It's harder to find a voice, and when you do, the level of interaction can seem small compared to other web copywriter tasks. This isn't negative and remember, each 'like' and 'share' represents an individual who wilfully engaged for a moment with your brand. And as social media grows so will its reach.

BLOGGING

What is a blog?

A blog is a **frequently** updated online personal journal or diary. It's a place to express yourself or your organisation to the world. A place to share your thoughts and passions – or in a corporate setting to share company news. Blog is a short form for the word web log and the two terms are used interchangeably.

Here are a couple of other definitions:

> *"...the first journalistic model that actually harnesses rather than merely exploits the true democratic nature of the web. It's a medium finally finding a unique voice."* – Andrew Sullivan

> *"[a] collection of posts ... short, informal, sometimes controversial, and sometimes deeply personal ... with the freshest information at the top."* – Meg Hourihan

Originally blogs were known as places for people to write about their day-to-day activities. Their mundane, everyday tasks became fodder for journal entries. Somehow these writers gained a following and the hobby of blogging was born. Today people write about far more interesting topics and above all companies identify good writers internally who can take often mundane issues and turn them into entertaining reading.

Galley Cat – one of the top publishing blogs

J.K. Rowling Declares Cursed Child to be the Final Harry Potter Story

-

-

-

By Maryann Yin on Aug. 1, 2016 – 9:00 AM Comment[7]

Over the weekend, the two-part Harry Potter and the Cursed Child *play officially opened in London's West End and the script book for this theatrical show was also released.* **J.K. Rowling** *has declared that this project, the eighth Harry Potter story, marks the conclusion of Harry Potter's story.*

According to the RadioTimes, Rowling gave this statement during a press event: "[Harry] goes on a very big journey during these two plays and then, yeah, I think we're done. This is the next generation, you know. So, I'm thrilled to see it realised so beautifully but, no, Harry is done now."

Vanity Fair *reports that although this heroic character's story may be finished, stories from the wizarding world will continue on with the* Fantastic Beasts and Where to Find Them *movie trilogy, Rowling's Pottermore essays, and Rowling's magical habit of sharing new information with her fans on Twitter. The first* Fantastic Beasts *film, scripted by Rowling herself, will hit theatres on November 18. (via Reuters)*

---

7   Yin, M. August, 1, 2016. .K. Rowling Declares Cursed Child to be the Final Harry Potter Story. *Galley Cat.* Retrieved from: https://www.adweek.com/galleycat/j-k-rowling-declares-cursed-child-to-be-the-final-harry-potter-story/123174

Critical re-thinking
Published July 26, 2016 by **Katy Guest**[8]

There's nothing like reading your own obituary to give a journalist a wake-up call.

Last month, The Bookseller editor Philip Jones published a lament on the demise of literary editors and, as one of those he mentioned – I edited The Independent on Sunday*'s books pages from 2009 until the paper's closure in March – I share his fears. Book reviews sections "are in mortal danger", he wrote, "and ....once they are gone, we will marvel at what we have lost".*

Unsurprisingly, I agree. While there remain some magnificent books sections that I cherish, the disappearance of any medium is a loss. Not only did The Independent on Sunday *help to discover fledgling writers (Sarah Waters, David Mitchell, Tasha Kavanagh, Hanya Yanagihara ...) and champion well-known ones (we published new writing by A L Kennedy, Louis de Bernières, Fay Weldon...), it did so while campaigning for gender equality in children's books and against the monopolisation of the industry by Amazon, and while maintaining a balance of male and female reviewers (an impossible task, according to some other publications). Until the end, we insisted on paying reviewers.*

Reviews by accountable, named reviewers are more important than ever in a world where every anonymous sock-puppets and their mother are imploring readers to shell out £18.99

Professional reviews by accountable, named reviewers are more important than ever in a world where every anonymous sock-puppet and their mother are imploring readers to shell out £18.99 on the latest five-star hardback. I recently spoke at a seminar for authors, where one told me that his publisher insists he asks

---

8   Guest. K. July, 26, 2016. Critical re-thinking. *The Booksellers.* Retrieved from: https://www.thebookseller.com/blogs/critical-re-thinking-369096

all of his friends and family to review him online. The magic number of reviews is 50, apparently, to trip some sort of algorithm.

There are, of course, some fantastic online reviewers, but doing a proper job is hard work. In May, the blogger Bookslut hung up her keyboard, admitting, "Running it takes a lot of time, and it makes no money … and when I realised the sacrifices I was going to have to make in order for it to make money, it wasn't worth it."

To a literary editor, that sounds familiar. In the seven years I did the job, my budget was cut by more than half. Book lovers complained about online clickbait, while even some publishers begrudged buying a copy of the paper for their office. As Jones noted, publishers seldom advertise in books sections. They told me that a review or interview was worth far more to them than any amount of advertising in the same space. An author friend confided that her publisher would rather pay for an intimate lunch for key critics than advertise in their publications. One such lunch would cost more than my entire weekly budget.

The closure of newspapers and books sections spells trouble for publishing, then, but I can see one silver lining: all the brilliant people who are now available for work as editors. Publishers ought to snap them up, because a former literary editor is exactly the person to help you make great books and sell lots of them.

We know about books (most of us received about 200 of them per week, by the sack full) and we have a nose for a story. As journalists, we know how to spot the next big thing, not just copy the last one.

We've already got to grips with "online". We have, in a pile of scruffy reporters' notebooks, an extensive network of contacts who can write. We've spent years meeting interesting people and hearing their stories (and ideas for books), and of course we have good friends in the media. We wouldn't claim that we can do the publicity department's job for them, but we can help.

What we're really good at, though, is editing: thoroughly, sensitively and in a hurry, whether the writing is by a Booker Prize-winning author or an unheard-of amateur with a good idea.

We can do all of this with a tiny, shrinking budget, and we never, ever miss a deadline. And you know that we're not in this business for the money, the glamour or the easy life; we just get a kick out of getting good books to happy readers.

Fortunately, literary editors are not quite dead yet. But publishers would be wise to invest in them, one way or another.

Katy Guest is the former editor of the books pages of The Independent on Sunday.

Helping your teenager decide what to do after school[9]

Having a teenager in your home, means you need to help them make wise decisions and I mean it when I say "help", not dictate to them what they must do. Planning your child's future is not something you should handle once they have finished school; it starts as soon as they start their matric year.

Being the parent isn't always an easy task, you need to know your child's interests and hobbies and know what they would want to study in future, so this all boils down to building the relationship with your children.

It can be difficult to imagine your baby as an adult, with the right approach, helping your teen make the transition into adulthood can be rewarding.

---

9   JobVine Industry Journal Blog. 4 February 2014. Retrieved from: http://www.jobvine.co.za/blog/2014/02/helping-your-teenager-decide-what-to-do-after-school/

Going to college, getting a job, or taking time off are the common choices your teen will likely face. Here's how you can help your adult-to-be make the best decision...

Here are tips to help your teenagers decide what's best for them and what they can do after school. Give your kids the options, don't force a choice of study on them; let them decide what they want to do. Some kids would prefer not studying for the first year after school, you can allow this but do not allow them to sit at home after school; give them 'gap-year' options as well, they should stay busy and active.

Remember, it's Your Teenager's Life

When the subject concerns the future, some teenagers may try to avoid it at all times. Here's how to get the ball rolling and keep communication flowing at all times:

- Listen to your teenager and resist the temptation to provide unsolicited advice. If your teen is struggling to make a decision, a story or two about a tough choice you had to make could be very reassuring.

- Provide respect and support while giving up some control. Trying to direct your teen's future probably won't be a benefit in the long run. This is the time for teens to develop decision-making and problem-solving skills.

- Prepare your teen to be self-sufficient away from home. This includes making major decisions regarding dating, drugs, alcohol, and sex, as well as mastering day-to-day living skills (cooking, cleaning, laundry, grocery shopping, paying bills, and managing a budget).

- Don't be afraid to set limits on how much you can financially support a teen who decides to take time off. It's important for teens to learn independence.

Where to Get Help

The Internet is a good starting point for researching information on your teenager's interests. Also enlist the help of school counsellors, who can help steer kids in the right direction or refer them to other good sources of information.

And don't overlook your local library. In addition to books and magazine articles on subjects of interest, the librarian can be a wealth of information.

Lastly, resist the temptation to lecture and try to remain supportive and enthusiastic, even if your teen keeps changing his or her mind. Your teen needs your positive influence during this transitional time.

Blogging traps and tips

Spelling and grammar errors

Once again proofread, spell check and then proofread again. **AND READ IT OUT LOUD**! Preview your post before you publish it. Even have someone else glance at it. Of course, we all make mistakes, but do your best to publish a post free of obvious errors. You have no idea how quickly some smart arse will come back at you.

Regurgitated content

If you said something that bears repeating, link back to that original post. Your readers will know if you keep spitting out the same old content and Google frowns upon duplicate posts. It's a bad idea all around.

Flashy backgrounds

Yuk. Black backgrounds with flashing lights and neon colours are not only hideous and hard to read, but they also take away what people are really at your blog to see: Great content.

Plagiarism (which I've done here a bit ...)

Don't steal someone else's words without giving them credit…

Filling a vacuum with your blog

Don't be a copy-cat and re-edit someone else's blog. Generate original content. This is a must in order to stand out from the crowd.

Lots of content

Quality certainly comes first. But if you want to have a successful blog, you need both.

Use plenty of pictures in your blog posts

No one wants to see endless blocks of text, especially while reading online. The moment your reader's mind wanders off, they'll be jumping to another site before you know it. Here are some great sources for finding images: Flickr, Photobucket, picapp, Google Image Search, Pinterest.

How often to blog?

There's no right answer here but try and stick to a regular time so people know when to look for your next blog – say every week. Don't start off thinking you can be witty and sharp every day.

Put an author section in your blog posts

No one wants to read material written by a faceless author, let alone by one without a name. Many companies use a side-bar with photos and names of their authors.

TWITTER[10]

There's no getting away from it – Twitter is growing by the minute and if your organisation isn't using it yet, they've almost missed the boat.

---

10 The Offbeat Story. [nd]. Twitter Marketing Tips – Engagement Stats. Retrieved from: http://www.theoffbeatstory.com/5-twitter-marketing-tips-to-drive-traffic-and-conversions/twitter-marketing-tips-engagement-stats-2/

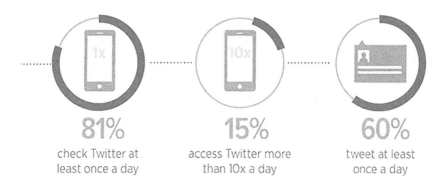

81%
check Twitter at
least once a day

15%
access Twitter more
than 10x a day

60%
tweet at least
once a day

Why read Twitter?

This is where people go to talk about what they care about and what's happening around them right now. In terms of business use it's an invaluable tool to promote, connect and brand a company.

If your company isn't using Twitter they're missing out on a massive marketing opportunity. Yes, you can only use 140 characters but the whole idea in terms of Tweeting for business is to try and send the reader to a link – either your blog or a specific news item on your website.

Getting such a short message across is often a case of trial and error. You don't realise how short 140 characters is until you try writing a Tweet. Research shows that Tweets shorter than 100 characters get a 17% higher engagement rate.

The best part is that you can add pictures and videos to your Tweets that make them more exciting and allow your audience to really engage with your brand.

Timing here is everything, especially when it comes to breaking news – or climbing on the back of breaking news. It all depends on what you're Tweeting about and who you want to reach. It's a case of trial and error to begin with.

Getting people to follow your Tweets

The secret here is to seek out the companies or individuals you want to follow you and follow them first. Very often, once they see they're being followed by you, they'll return the compliment.

A lot of companies today employ a social media team just to monitor their Facebook and Twitter, amongst others. This means they can connect with their customers in real time.

Bolden important words

Another way to help users locate information quickly and easily is to bolden important words in some paragraphs. When site visitors scan through the screen this text stands out, so make sure the text makes sense out of context.

Bolden two to three words which **describe the main point** of the paragraph, and not words on which you're placing emphasis. By seeing these boldened words site visitors can instantly understand what the paragraph's about and decide whether or not they want to read it.

 EXERCISE

Put sub-headings into the following article:

Unit trusts

For the "man on the street" or for the well-seasoned investor, unit trusts offer a simple and effective way of saving money – they are also the perfect way to build a balanced and diversified investment portfolio, with exposure to the stock exchange. Unit trusts allow a large group of people to pool their capital for investment in the equity, bond and money markets. This gives investors affordable access to investment professionals, who will manage the pool of capital according to set mandates and varying risk profiles.

STANLIB was established in 2002 and is wholly owned by the Liberty Group, following a merger of the Liberty and Standard Bank Group's asset management, wealth management and unit trust businesses. This served to cement a history of collaboration that began in the 1960s. As one of South Africa's top investment managers, STANLIB has received numerous awards for investment performance.

We have an experienced team of top investment professionals managing a broad range of local and global equity investments. Our range of products also includes onshore and offshore targeted return and balanced funds that combine a range of asset classes in one portfolio, offering our clients risk- and-return-appropriate investment funds.

 **EXERCISE**

Write a short paragraph highlighting key words on what your company does. Give it a headline.

| |
| |
| |
| |
| |
| |
| |
| |
| |
| |

CONCLUSION

In my work I engage with many different types of organisations from government and parastatal to large corporations and smaller companies. Over the last few years what has emerged as the most pressing issue in all of these when it comes to communication is reluctance to embrace the digital world.

When you're dealing with people today, whether internal or external, one thing they all have in common is where they go to get their information – at speed. The internet – encompassing social media, emails, Google, Facebook and more. As I've shown in the book, people's attention span has shrunk, so whether you're trying to get your staff to read a newsletter or your clients to stay on your website, you have a small gap in which to grab and hold their attention.

Hopefully, after reading this book, you will feel more inclined to dive further into the digital world and see how this can make your life easier. After all, wouldn't you be proud to be one of the first organisations to have a totally digital Annual General Report that would actually be of use to people and take just 10 or 15 minutes to 'listen' to. So don't be afraid of change – rather welcome the opportunity to do things differently. The rewards will be great.

REFERENCES

Andrews, L. 29 March 2017. #Bookmarks2017: Digital download with ... Honeykome. Bizcommunity. Retrieved from: http://www.bizcommunity.com/Article/196/459/159708.html

Bizcommunity.com. 29 March 2017. *Daredevil Run collects R500,000 for CANSA.* Retrieved from: http://www.bizcommunity.com/Gallery/196/40/4281.html.html

Chen, J., Hyde, J., Yaemsaard, N. & Yang, T. 2009. Situation Analysis – Hilton in China. Retrieved from: https://www.slideshare.net/jlw264/hilton-situation-analysis-14221254

Dinosauriens.info. 2018. 6 Tips on Creating Compelling Newsletter Titles Writtent. My Posters. Retrieved from: http://dinosauriens.fo/?u=6+Tips+on+Creating+Compelling+Newsletter+Titles++Writtent

Guest. K. July, 26, 2016. Critical re-thinking. *The Booksellers.* Retrieved from: https://www.thebookseller.com/blogs/critical-re-thinking-369096

JobVine Industry Journal Blog. 4 February 2014. Retrieved from: http://www.jobvine.co.za/blog/2014/02/helping-your-teenager-decide-what-to-do-after-school/

Knowler, W. 2016. Ford confirms Kuga fires confined to single model, concedes engine overheating a possible cause. Times Live. Retrieved from: https://www.timeslive.co.za/news/consumer-live/2016-12-22-ford-confirms-kuga-fires-confined-to-single-model-concedes-engine-overheating-a-possible-cause/

Makhumbila, J. 3 March 2017. Free Bicycles for Primary School Learners. City of Ekurhuleni. Retrieved from: https://www.ekurhuleni.gov.za/yourservices/news/press-releases/free-bicycles-for-primary-school-learners

Naidu-Hoffmeester, R., & Hanekom, J. (nd). Bridging the distance in distance education. Unisa News & Media. Retrieved from: http://www.unisa.ac.za/sites/corporate/default/News-&-Media/Articles/Bridging-the-distance-in-distance-education

Schontal, M. 8 December 2015. Nokia's internal communication driven by social media. Simplycommunicate. Retrieved from: https://simply-communicate.com/nokias-internal-communication-driven-social-media/

The DTI Media Statement. February, 2017. Fuel Cell Bus Workshop Whets Appetite of SA Cities. Retrieved from: https://www.thedti.gov.za/editmedia.jsp?id=3965

The Offbeat Story. [nd]. Twitter Marketing Tips – Engagement Stats. Retrieved from: http://www.theoffbeatstory.com/5-twitter-marketing-tips-to-drive-traffic-and-conversions/twitter-marketing-tips-engagement-stats-2/

Yin, M. August, 1, 2016. J.K. Rowling Declares Cursed Child to be the Final Harry Potter Story. Galley Cat. Retrieved from: https://www.adweek.com/galleycat/j-k-rowling-declares-cursed-child-to-be-the-final-harry-potter-story/123174

INDEX